Do-It-Yourself Family

Do-It-Yourself Family

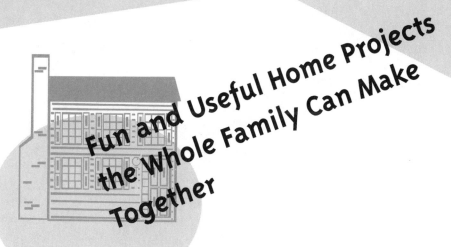

Fun and Useful Home Projects the Whole Family Can Make Together

Written and Illustrated by
Eric Stromer

Bantam Books

DO-IT-YOURSELF FAMILY
A Bantam Book

Published by Bantam Dell
A Division of Random House, Inc.
New York, New York

Book design by Glen M. Edelstein

Bantam Books and the rooster colophon are registered trademarks
of Random House, Inc.

ISBN-13: 978-0-553-38402-4
ISBN-10: 0-553-38402-3

Printed in the United States of America

DEDICATED TO Amy, Wyatt, and Dusty. Thank you
for teaching me to be a better man.

And to Erv, Sally, and Kurt, thanks for making my
childhood such a blast.

To Sheryl and Yfat, thanks for making this project rock.
And to Peter and Philip, thanks for making it roll!

Contents

I.
The
Do-It-Yourself
Family Dream
Team

I HAVE OFTEN thought of family life as a great unwinnable battle, complete with strategies, battle plans, troop movements, victories, and of course, occasional total and complete failure and humiliation.

For any who disagree, try loading a family of four (two children, ages two and seven) into a car with an imposed time limit (morning car pool!) and tell me you're not engaged in a major military operation. And do I even need to mention getting the kids to clean up their rooms? *I didn't think so.* What about that great and elusive mystery of the ages—quality family time? If your home is anything like mine, *quality* is on the endangered list.

On the other hand, I am fortunate enough to have met a woman who, in a moment of insanity, decided to accept my marriage proposal, and then willingly bore my beautiful, yet sometimes challenging, children. The topper is that Amy remains true to her principles as the center and strength of our family unit.

After seeing my home disintegrate into total chaos one too many times, our crazy experiences encouraged me to jot down a few useful ideas for home and hearth improvement. Once put in place, these solutions didn't exactly transform our home overnight, but they've made a huge difference in the way we enjoy one another. Interested? *Thought so.* Read on for my personal DIY Family Dream Team solutions for every room in the house!

CREATING THE DREAM TEAM

My notion to involve the family in my home improvement plans came to me as my son Dusty entertained himself by hurling his brother's toys at my head. Meanwhile, my older son, Wyatt—the rightful owner of said toys—was screaming that he didn't have anything to play with. Suddenly, I thought—*voilà!*—if my kids have so much free time, why not train them to serve as my very own Dream Team?

After all, doing hands-on projects together was how I got to really know *my* dad. Sure, he said many things to me, but none resonated more than when we were together building stuff. We didn't even need to talk; but the more we worked together, the more I gained a sense of who he was and who I wanted to be. Based on this experience, what evolved was a desire to draw my family closer through projects we could make together.

Plus, because my wife and I have such hectic professional lives, we made a joint decision not to allow our home to be overrun by super-slick commercial messages from media and commerce—particularly aimed at our children through kids' programming. Instead, we turned off the tube and slowed down the pace with some good old-fashioned woodworking. Our age-appropriate projects were born. My seven-year-old, Wyatt, could obviously handle more involved tasks than my toddler could. But don't count out the mighty Dusty Stromer! I found that he could handle some hand-sanding, painting, and of course, the ever-popular picking up the spilled screws that Dad kicked over. I reveled in how much quality time we were having together, all the while producing something that would continue to serve our home life long after the project was completed. Sort of like *construction* and *crafting* meets *day care*.

I knew I could get my wife on board. Any interest in fixing up, organizing, or renovating our home gets me far more points than a fancy night out or a two-week getaway to a tropical paradise. It wasn't Amy I was worried about—it was *the boys*! My guys have two speeds: on and off. How would I get my little band of insurgents to comply?

In the case of my family, I managed to get my kids to participate in executing my home-improvement ideas by using two key strategies. One: make the project fun, so that it combats the boredom factor. Two: include the kids in all the aspects of making the house work, so that they feel a sense of ownership in the project and its continued use.

Making the Project Fun. Ever heard of the Family Theory of Relativity? This long-accepted principle of family science (in which I have a Ph.D., did I tell you?) basically stands for the proposition that when left to their own devices, your smallest relatives (i.e., kids) will ultimately run out of things to do. This is where the "Dad, I'm bored" problem pops up. Over and over again. In stereo. And high-definition. Having a stash of fun home-improvement ideas at the ready remedies this problem in a flash. And suddenly everyone is entertained and happy. My kids never do anything simply because they're supposed to—they do things because they *want* to.

Allowing Your Kids to Take Ownership of the Solution. Freedom of speech is great in theory, except when your toddler keeps babbling, "Daddy, where's my soccer ball?" "Daddy, where's my baseball bat?" "Daddy, where's my . . . ?" The "Daddy, where is" game is never-ending. Twenty minutes of this torture is all I can take. But once I enlisted my boys' efforts in creating the storage unit that houses their unused sports equipment, they easily answered their *own* questions, because they had enthusiastically put away their soccer ball in the first place. In other words, giving them a stake in the process of organization caused them to become willing participants and coconspirators!

CREATING YOUR DREAM TEAM

Here are ten top-secret tips for keeping your troops motivated to finish once the project is under way:

1. Keep it fun.
2. Keep it simple.
3. Involve everyone, no matter what the age.
4. If the kids lose focus, give them something else to do. Mix it up!
5. Honor creativity and ingenuity; they *may* know how to do it better!
6. Don't be afraid to improvise.
7. Don't rush to finish. It's about the journey, not the destination.
8. Don't forget the snacks and beverages. There's nothing worse than a cranky little woodworker with low blood sugar.
9. Don't allow the kids to compete.
10. Praise all things way too much. Who doesn't need an extra dose of self-esteem?

SETTING MY PLAN TO ACTION

Did my Dream Team come together right away? Sort of. What followed was a period of trial and error, with some false starts. And then, believe it or not, the kids actually started coming to me. They came *before* they got bored. And they had ideas of their own regarding what they wanted to build.

Keeping Them Interested

My house is traditionally a place where all the neighborhood kids like to hang out. This is because the Stromers are always doing something interesting. My wife and I love kids. But more than that, creativity and self-expression are really honored in the Stromer home, whether it is building a new storage system for Mom or making the world's coolest tent for the kids. We always have fun projects going on. As a dad, it also makes me feel more comfortable having my own kids where I can see them. Not to mention the added benefit of enlisting the services of the neighborhood kids to help us with our projects. Think of the old Pennsylvania Dutch tradition of barn building. Once one comes, they all come.

Holy harmonious home life!

The rebel fighters responded. Toys were being put away in record time. Kids were coming over and playing with a purpose! All I had to do was feed them, give them a project to do, and behold, stuff started getting done around the house! Domestic bliss was mine! I, Eric Stromer, did not suck! Self-esteem flowed like chocolate milk! Shortly thereafter, this book was born.

SAFETY FIRST

When working with tools of any kind, it is imperative to make safety your number one priority! Doing so will encourage your kids to do the same. Always wear safety glasses when cutting, sawing, chipping, screwing, hammering, etc. Never wear gloves when operating power tools as they can become tangled in the rotating parts of the tool. Always lift materials with bent knees and a straight back. Never work when you are tired, angry, lonely, or sad.

Avoid even simple distractions while using tools. In the name of safety, make like those obnoxious Hollywood types and use your "personal assistants" to do things for you that any other self-respecting human would do for themselves. For example, don't attempt to tie your own shoes, let your kids help you (but put down the power tools first!). *Tee-hee.*

Hearing protection is key.

What?

See, that's what I'm saying. You must wear hearing protection when hammering or using power tools that make loud noises.

OUTFITTING YOUR TOOLBOX

I am a tool junkie! I love the way the *right* tool can make an impossible job a piece of cake. For this reason, even beginner DIY Families may wish to spend a few extra minutes in the tool aisle.

Depending on your ambition and the types of projects you plan to undertake, there are two levels of toolboxes you can build: the basic and primo versions. I have also made a few recommendations for *ultra*-primo additional tools you may wish to invest in to round out your collection.

The basic toolbox includes:

Tool belt
Work gloves
Slot head screwdriver
Phillips head screwdriver
16-ounce hammer
Nail set
Locking pliers
Long nose pliers
Wire stripper
Wire cutters
Tape measure

Stud finder

Torpedo level

Socket wrench

Allen wrench set

8" adjustable crescent wrench

Handsaw

Mini hacksaw

Utility knife

Tin snip

1½" putty knife

Paintbrushes

Paint rollers

Paint roller trays

Pencil

Chalk/chalk line

Indelible black marker

Safety glasses or goggles for you, your Dream Team, and a few spares
for the neighborhood kids

The primo version includes all of the above, plus:

Power drill/screwdriver

Reciprocating saw

Circular saw

Table saw

Nail gun and compressor (my personal favorite)

BUYING AND USING YOUR TOOLS AND ACCESSORIES

There are many choices when it comes to purchasing tools. I list my favorites below. If you're just entering the tool market, there are simplified options depending on your skill level. This brief overview will give you some idea of what you may want, and why. Keep in mind this list gives you options in terms of price range, power, and style. Choose the product that works within your budget, skill range, and individual needs.

Tool Belt

First, and foremost, you gotta have the **tool belt**. Even if you never do anything around your house in terms of remodeling, just to wear this thing feels cool! When my kids were babies, I would wear my tool belt with a bottle in one pouch and a diaper, a cell phone, a few toys, and a pacifier in the other. For around $22 to $35 you can get a great twelve-pocket suede tool belt.

Work Gloves

Look for **work gloves** that have *leather* palms and fingertips, or *synthetic* gloves that are really cool but a bit more expensive. Try on a few pairs and see which provide you with the most freedom of movement, and with a little protection as well. Please don't wear gloves when working with saws and drills. You really need to feel power tools when operating them. I use gloves for protection, not tool operation. You can get a great pair of work gloves for $2 to $12.

Hammer

The hammer is the first tool to get if you don't already have one. They come in all shapes and sizes. There are **finish**, **framing**, and **sledge hammers**. I love the hammer! It's the most simple and effective tool ever invented. You can hit stuff, pull nails out of walls, and demolish and break stuff all for $5 to $40.

The key to the right size hammer is your ability to control it. If it's too light, you won't generate enough power to drive in a nail. If it's too heavy, you won't be able to control it, and you'll never be able to hit the nail on its head! That's when a hammer gets dangerous.

For kids, I recommend a **7-ounce starter claw hammer**. It's light enough for a five-year-old to swing with control and accuracy. Kid-size hammers are around $2 to $5.

For an adult starter hammer, try a **10-** to **20-ounce claw hammer**, which costs between $5 and $30. As you peruse the available hammers, swing each one using downward "hammering" motions and see how it feels. Your ideal hammer should feel substantial enough to drive a nail but not so heavy that it could fly out of your hand. If you feel like you can handle something slightly heavier, go for it! You need to know that the only thing you gain in a heavier hammer is power; but that's only half the story when it comes to hammering. Finesse and agility are key.

If you're interested in hammering large lumber (2 x 4s or larger) you may want to consider a **framing hammer**, usually weighing between 19 and 28 ounces. They are specially designed for driving longer nails into larger pieces of wood. They sometimes also have a waffle-iron head to grip the nail a little better when hammering. Ergonomically, they are beautifully shaped to make force and power as comfortable as possible when slamming a 3" nail into a huge piece of wood. Framing hammers cost between $20 and $40.

Power Drill/Screwdriver

The general rule with power tools is that the more expensive the item, the more power you get. The amount of power is reflected in the higher number of amps for tools with cords attached, and volts for cordless power products.

To test a tool, ask to try out any of the **power drills/screwdrivers**, from **7 to 18 volts**, at your nearest big home improvement store. Bring a piece of scrap wood with you and try screwing in a 1" and then a 3" drywall screw. Your tool should feel powerful and easy to use without having to put too much downward pressure on the screw head. Note that the more powerful drills/screwdrivers are usually larger in size. Get the highest volume of volts you can physically control in your hand and that you can afford. Power drills/screwdrivers range in price from $30 to $250.

For kids, the **7-volt screw gun** is easily manageable. Unfortunately, you don't get much power with such a small drill/screwdriver. For this reason, only buy this smaller tool if you plan on using it as a tool with which to involve your young kids in the process of drilling or screwing.

A **compact screw guide** with assorted tips (Phillips head or slot, $5) inserts into your power drill/screwdriver, slides down around the screw, and magnetically holds the screw on the tip no matter how long it is, then retracts as you screw into the wood. It is an amazingly helpful add-on.

Finally, invest in, at minimum, a **13-piece drill bit set** ($10). This set gives you a wide choice of drilling possibilities, with drill bit sizes adequate for all the projects we will do in this book.

Additional Power Tools

Power tools are my absolute favorite category. There is literally a tool for every need. Here are a few of my favorites for woodworking projects.

The **7 1/4" circular saw** gives you the ability to crosscut 2 x 4s like a hot knife through butter. Well . . . if butter tasted like a piece of milled pine. Anyway, you catch my drift. There are many reasons to own one of these bad boys. First of all, as an all-purpose wood-cutting tool for larger size lumber (1 x 2 and up to 4 x 12 beams) there is no substitute. This saw is also a good choice for cutting a long run of plywood freehand. It's versatile and handles multipurpose cutting tasks with ease. This saw requires some skill to operate and is definitely not recommended for kids under age twelve. The saws range from $50 to $200. Again, the more powerful the saw, the more money you will spend. For example, the higher the rating of amps or volts, the more powerful the tool is. I like the saws that have a longer body style for cutting straight on a long cut.

The **jigsaw** is great because you can cut curves with it. It has a reciprocating blade that moves up and down rapidly, much like a sewing machine needle. With any of the projects in the book that call for cutting curving designs or circular cutouts, the jigsaw is your baby. I personally picked up a 5-amp jigsaw for around $140 and love it! If you plan on adding your own creative touches to the designs, please get a jigsaw. It will make woodworking self-expression a snap!

The **10" chop saw** is used for cutting trim, molding, wood dowel curtain rods, 2 x 4s, and short jobs like shelving lengths. If you want to create tricky crown molding details, nothing beats the compound miter version of the chop saw. The compound miter version allows the saw to pivot right and left at varying degrees and gives you the ability to tackle any project requiring complicated angles. The chop saw will run between $100 and $500.

The **10" table saw** is ideal for tackling multiple projects requiring long, straight, perfect cuts. This saw is a must for cabinet and furniture makers. The table saw also makes cutting long, 8' rips out of a 4'x 8' sheet of plywood a snap! This type of saw will cost you between $100 and $300. Well worth the investment when you consider a desk, shelving system, or any store-bought item could easily exceed $300 and doesn't afford you the added benefit of saying, "Yeah, I built this cool bed with my daughter." Honestly, how do you put a price tag on that?

The **router** is a woodworking tool used to hollow out (or *rout*) an area in the face of a piece of wood or to carve edge details. Routers use a *collet*, which is an adjustable collar that secures the router bit into the unit. Common *collet* capacities run from 1/4" to 1/2". The larger the capacity, the greater the variety of size of router bits you can use. How would you use this? If, for example, you want your Mini-Viking Kitchen Center (see page 101) to have a rounded detail on all the edges, instead of sanding all the corners off of the wood by hand, you could run the router along all of your edges to quickly and easily round off the wood. Virtually any detail you can think of is possible to create more efficiently with a router. This is another great tool with which to express your creativity. Routers range in price from $50 to $200.

The **5" orbital sander** is great for cutting your sanding time down to nothing, for roughly $35. This sanding tool vibrates, rotates, and comes equipped with 5" replaceable sanding disks that attach to the tool with either Velcro or adhesive. I love the random orbital sander because it's a great starter power tool for kids four and older. With minimal coaching you can train even the kid with the shortest attention span *ever* to focus. Just make sure they wear a dust mask and safety glasses!

The **nail gun** is my favorite tool and soon will be yours. Oh boy, what can I say? This tool makes life worth living. The nail gun enables you to *shoot* nails into wood using an air compression tank system. It puts all the fun into constructing projects. You just place the tip of the gun where you want to nail and gently press it into your nail surface, pull the trigger, and BLAM! You've just shot a nail into a piece of wood.

This tool shoots nails up to 3$1/2$" long. For our purposes, a $120, 2", 18-gauge brad nailer will do the trick. If you feel like you want a little more power, you could go to the 2$1/2$" finish nailer for $200.

A Word About Safety. While it's true that whenever you use this baby you feel like a secret agent on a secret mission to do secret things, and that *every time* you shoot a nail you will feel that you've made the world just a little bit better for all of us (thanks, by the way), the fact is that this tool is definitely not a toy! The nail gun requires supervising adults to be completely confident in their abilities with the nail gun. Never let a kid under twelve operate the nail gun unsupervised by an adult. I don't recommend letting kids under eight even try the nail gun. Safety glasses are a must for everyone standing around the project area (bearing witness to the awe-inspiring beauty that is the nail gun), *even* if they are just watching. Having said all this, remember that when properly used, the nail gun is by far the most fun you will ever have in your whole life! Well . . . maybe not the *most* fun, but more fun than just about 97.75% of the stuff you usually do.

An **air compressor** is necessary for powering the nail gun. Air compressors can also blow up basketballs, bicycle tires, pool toys, and car tires; blow off sawdust from your work areas; sweep off your driveway;

My brother, Kurt, and I used to mess around with our Schwinn Sting-Ray bicycles. Our parents introduced us to tools when we were very young. We were able to use tools to create and experiment with freedom and ease. We spent hours modifying our bikes—hacksawing and screwing and bolting and drilling.

My parents could easily get two and a half hours of unsupervised babysitting time out of those bikes, just by letting us work in our basement workshop. To us, that small basement of our Evanston apartment was the place where anything was possible.

My whole family was into building stuff. My parents were serial room rearrangers and decorators. The apartment we rented was a blank canvas for interior design. They always said when we move, we'll have to paint it back to white, so why not make it as cool as we can right now? The Stromers weren't exactly swimming in do-re-mi, but what we lacked in finances, we made up for in creativity!

My brother and I were recruited to assist in this home improvement how-to. By the time I was five, I was wallpapering, painting, and (I don't mind saying) developing a flair for interior design. By the time I left for college I had remodeled my room about twelve times.

In retrospect, the various versions of my childhood bedroom reflected my own development over the years—every change evidenced a new interest that was going on in my world. I also believe that actively participating in the creation of my room encouraged me to keep my room clean and neat because I had spent my free time creating a hangout space that suited my tastes and needs! And the reason I experienced this benefit was that I had been introduced to working with tools at a young age.

I have passed this lesson on to my older son, Wyatt. The younger one still calls me "Mommy," so I don't think he's quite able to grasp these concepts yet. As parents, the more you know what tools can do and how to safely use them, the better.

and, my favorite, blow your hair back like you're in a photo shoot power-posing your way to international superstardom!

I like the 6-gallon jobsite air compressor. The larger ones take too long to fill up. The 6-gallon air compressor will cost anywhere from $200 to $350. Well worth it for the full nail-gun experience.

Plywood

The basis of most of the projects in this book is plywood. I specifically suggest birch plywood because it is the least expensive and best looking choice out there. Plywood comes in a standard 4' x 8' sheet or a one-half sheet, which is 4' x 4'. What varies most in plywood is the thickness. The average cost for a sheet of 3/4" thick birch plywood is $35. Most of the projects in this book use either 1/2" or 3/4" thickness. The materials list will call for the size and type of plywood as *one sheet of plywood, 3/4" thick* or *one-half sheet of plywood, 1/2" thick*. Just know that one sheet is 4' x 8' and a one-half sheet is 4' x 4'. Luan is a great choice for a backing on a cabinet because it is very inexpensive and easy to work with. Think of it as a finish-grade plywood that requires little or no prep for finishing.

Measuring Tools

A **25' tape measure** costs around $8.50 and is the perfect adult size and the ideal length for nearly every project. It easily fits in the tape measure pocket of all tool belts. See illustrations on page 16 for easy measuring how-tos.

For kids, a **12' tape measure** for about $8 is the perfect kid size.

Another great measuring tool that fits easily in your tool belt is the **7" rafter square,** or **speed square,** as I like to call it. It's a triangle-shaped measuring tool that can give you right angles off any straight-edged piece of wood you work with and can also help you figure out angles if you need to. As an alternative, look at a **12" combination square** to see if that design is more appealing to you. For what we're

How to Accurately Read a Tape Measure or Ruler

Admittedly, for the first year of my professional contracting career I used the old Egyptian method of hand and foot approximations when measuring out large-scale room additions. Sounds shaky, I know, but the fact is that my own foot is indeed 12¼". The reality is that when I used a regulation contractor's tape measure, I would "call" the measurement as 6" and 2-lines-shy-of-half-an-inch instead of 6⅜". This was because I didn't know the proper delineation for ¹⁄₁₆", ⅛", ¼", ½", and so on. It wasn't very accurate. Out of necessity I learned to read a tape measure, and you can, too!

¹⁄₁₆"

⅛"

³⁄₁₆"

¼"

⁵⁄₁₆"

⅜"

⁷⁄₁₆"

½"

⁹⁄₁₆"

⅝"

¹¹⁄₁₆"

¾"

¹³⁄₁₆"

⅞"

¹⁵⁄₁₆"

1"

going to do in this book, either square would be adequate. I like the speed square because it fits in my belt easier. They're both around $7.

Another great way to transpose long lines onto walls, floors, ceilings, or large plywood sheets is by using a **100' metal chalk line**.

This device is probably one of my kids' favorite tools. The chalk line is a palm-size metal container filled with blue, yellow, red, or white powdered chalk. A 100' string is wound up inside of it. Holding the line taut against the wall, you snap the line. You can create up to a 100', perfectly straight, colored chalk line just like that. Go on, try it. I dare you. It will be one of the single most enjoyable experiences of your lifetime! A chalk line with chalk is only about $7.50. Just get one! You'll see why after you do it just once.

Keeping It Level

Levels are amazing tools. They allow you to find a perfect *level* (horizontal) line or a perfect *plumb* (vertical) line. Around the house, a torpedo level or a 24" level is a perfect choice. The **torpedo level** fits in your tool belt because it's only 9" long. It's great to find level for hanging pictures, cabinets, or shelves. And because it's so small, you can whip it out of your tool belt while using your free hand to hold up the picture of me you're trying to hang on the wall. Place the torpedo level on the top of the frame, look for the little air bubble to center between the two lines, and scream, "I know it's level, it's the house that must be sinking to one side!" The torpedo level costs around $3.

The **24" level** is great because the additional length gives you a much more accurate reading over a greater distance. Say, for example, you want to mark a 4' line on the wall to denote the position of a shelf I'm going to soon teach you how to hang. By using the longer 24" level, you will get a much more accurate line positioning your level twice on the wall rather than trying to position nearly six lengths of the 9" torpedo level.

Levels come in 2" lengths all the way up to 6' lengths. Any longer and you move to a **laser level** or a **string line** with a small 2" line level attached to your span of string. A 24" level will run you about $6.50.

Stud Finder

To locate a stud (a vertical 2 x 4 piece of wood in your wall) in order to securely hang a heavy picture (over 60 pounds) or any heavy shelving or cabinetry, you may want to purchase a **stud finder**. This is not a dating service, but rather a battery-operated device that identifies where wood framing is located behind the wall. There is usually a piece of vertical wood framing every 16" inside your walls. Nailing or screwing into these points assures you have substantial wood framing to hold up whatever you choose to hang. You can get a decent stud finder for $12.

A Word of Warning. Sometimes stud finders can be misleading depending on the way your house was constructed. For example, if your walls are not drywall and wood framing, as most newer homes are, you may get inaccurate readings. Traditional plaster and lath walls found in older homes (1960 and before) can throw off the accuracy of a stud finder.

Glue

In nearly every instruction that involves fastening one piece of wood to another, you will see an instruction to *apply a bead of* **carpenter's glue** *to one or both edges before putting the sections together and screwing or nailing into place*. The reason for this is, believe it or not, that the strength of the glue (not nails or screws) provides 70% of the strength to your assembled piece. So, when you read the instructions that say "glue then screw" or "glue then nail," you'll not only know how but *why* you should never skip the glue. A 7.6-fluid-ounce bottle of glue will cost you a whopping $2.50.

Drywall Anchors

Drywall anchors come in plastic and metal versions. I prefer the metal versions as they support more weight when hanging items off of dry-

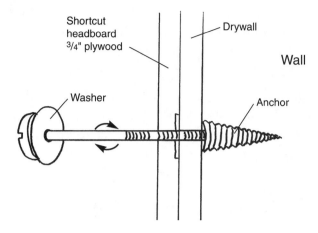

Shortcut headboard 3/4" plywood

Drywall

Wall

Washer

Anchor

wall. They are a simple solution for worry-free attachment of things to drywall. Drywall anchors come in two pieces: an anchor and a screw. Position the anchor at the end of your screwdriver bit, attached to your power drill/screwdriver. Gently place the tip of the anchor on the drywall at the desired location.

Ease back on the trigger and watch in amazement as the anchor rotates and buries itself into position. What you are left with is a screwhole receptacle that you will drill the screw into. You can either drill in the screw and leave 1/4" of the head out to hang pictures from, or you can screw through the item you wish to attach to the wall and securely hold it by snugging the screw into position.

Wood Dough or Plastic Wood

To fill in nail and screw holes, use a 4-ounce can of **wood dough** or **plastic wood**. This product comes in colors to match the type of wood you're using. Once it dries, it sands like wood, which is why I like it.

Nail and screw holes become virtually undetectable after filling them with this fast-drying miracle paste. A bit of warning for kids: it is oil-based and dries rapidly on little fingers, so use with caution. Removing this product requires using paint thinner, a chemical that will be absorbed by the skin. For old, bitter, and jaded adult skin and bodies, that's not a problem . . . but for little kids under age eight, it's better not to have them use this product.

Apply wood dough or plastic wood with a 1½" **putty knife**, pressing it into the hole and scraping off the excess. My preference is to use my fingers for application, then scrape off the excess with the putty knife. It feels like buttering toast with a hard piece of butter. My own personal nightmare, but that's how it feels, O.K.?

Caulk Gun and Caulk

If you're planning on painting (rather than staining) your projects, I recommend you fill in all the visible seams of your piece with a **caulk gun** and a tube of **white acrylic caulk**. The two will cost under $5. Insert the tube of caulk into the gun, snip off the end of the tube with a utility knife or scissors. Poke the seal, if necessary, to release the caulk. Press the nozzle to the crack and start filling by squeezing the trigger.

It's best to start at the edge of the crack away from you and work toward you. You'll learn this by trial and error, but you want to stop pulling the trigger on the caulk gun about 6" *before* you want to stop dispensing the product. Once you have laid down a line of caulk, wipe the excess off with your finger. Start at the point away from you and slide your finger toward you, scraping up the excess caulk. Wipe the caulk off onto a wet rag. Make one last pass lightly over the seam with the wet rag, in one direction. *Voilà!* The perfect seam. Just paint over the caulk and you'll never know a seam was there in the first place.

Your kids will stand in line for a crack at the caulk gun. And why not? It's a "gun" that squirts gooey stuff—what's more fun than that? This is an appropriate activity for kids ages seven and up. Caulk washes right off with warm soapy water. So don't worry! It is, however, a little difficult to get out of clothes once it sets so make sure no one is caulking in their Sunday best.

Sandpaper

No matter how much of a perfectionist you are, every wood project will need some sanding before it can be declared finished. Sanding is the great leveler: it will disguise the small differences between where two pieces of wood meet, improve the look of the wood grain, and make your project smooth and splinter-free. The basic technique is to always sand with the grain of the wood.

Sandpaper comes in varying degrees of coarseness—kind of like teenagers. The higher the number, the smoother and less abrasive the paper will be—kind of like parents. A paper of 220 grit and up will act more like a "polishing paper," smoothing out any rough spots of wood. A grit 120 or below will really knock off corners and differences in levels where two pieces of wood meet. If your project only requires cosmetic transformation, like feeling smoother to the touch or smoother for finish or paint, go with 220 grit. If you want to change angles or the structure slightly go with the 120 or lower. A box of 220 grit sandpaper contains twenty 9" x 11" sheets and runs about $8.50/box.

Sanding for Kids. Sanding is a great activity for kids. Those as young as six can easily pitch in on sanding detail. Sanding doesn't require razor-sharp hand-eye coordination, is relatively safe, and expends a great deal of energy. Some recommended safety gear includes a simple **paper dust mask**, if sanding for extended periods of time, and a pair of **child-size work gloves**.

Masking Tape and Duct Tape

I love tape! I'll scream it out loud in front of hundreds of strangers! Tape makes me feel like there *will* be a tomorrow. And at $4.50 per roll, duct tape is the world's greatest bargain! It's incredibly strong and can fasten together almost anything temporarily. Please run out and buy some right now!

Blue Painter's Tape

To mask off areas while I'm painting, I always use the blue colored masking tape, also called **painter's tape**. I choose the 1¹/₂" width. Any wider and you lose the necessary control to create a straight edge; also, the tape roll becomes too cumbersome to work with. Blue tape provides a clean paint line and yet can be removed cleanly and easily up to fourteen days after application. This means it won't stick too much to your surfaces, damage the finish or paint, or leave sticky tape gum on any surface you're working on. It's great to mask off areas where you don't want to paint. I use painter's tape for striping, color changes, and taping plastic sheathing or paper to walls and floors. The cost, approximately $6 to $7 per roll, is well worth it.

Paint Drip Protection

Nothing beats **red rosin paper** to protect hardwood, cement, or tile floors. It comes in a 166'-roll for about $11 to $13 and will protect and absorb spills well. Roll it out and tape it down with blue painter's tape.

Plastic sheathing is great for protecting carpet from paint drips and spills, but make sure to buy a drop cloth at least 2 millimeters thick; otherwise, it will tear easily. A 9' x 12' drop cloth is only $4. If you need more, you can buy a roll of 10' x 100' for $40.

A Note on Safety with Plastic. Make sure the younger kids don't play in or around large sheets of thick plastic. They can get tangled up in it and have a difficult time getting out.

To cut plastic to size, use a **utility knife** ($4). I like the type with the retractable blade because it is safe around kids as long as the blade is retracted. Remember, it's up to you to make sure it is!

Latex glove to look like rooster head!

Latex glove slips all the way over face

Not

Plastic Gloves

If you want to protect your hands from paint, stain, etc., pick up a box of disposable plastic gloves for $6.50 to $8. Plastic gloves are also fun to blow up and put on the top of your head. You will look just like a rooster! Again, only do this when supervised by an adult—or when trying to stop your little one from throwing a tantrum. It works great.

A Note on Safety with Plastic Gloves. Be aware that a glove can easily cover a kid's face when performing the rooster gag. Use caution! Sometimes comedy can be dangerous.

Clean-up Rags

For quick cleanup of paint spills, I like to have a box of rags on hand. You can get 200 easy-to-use, pop-up paper rags in a box for around $9 to $11. Well worth it!

Paintbrushes

For painting, staining, finishing, and priming my choice is the **angled sash brush**.

For kids, I like the **1¹/₂" nylon/polyester blend** for acrylic paints and stains, at $8 to $9. For adults, I like the **2¹/₂" nylon/polyester blend** for acrylic paints and stains, at $12 to $14. Kids can use little **2¹/₂ quart buckets** to hold paint at $2 per bucket.

Paint and Paintbrush Cleanup

To clean paintbrushes, purchase a $2 stainless-steel brush. Hold the paintbrush under running water and use the stainless-steel brush to comb the paint out of the brush on all four sides. Squirt a little dishwashing soap on the brush and keep combing away from the handle, until the water runs clear. After you're done, place the brush between your palms and roll your hands back and forth rapidly, like you're a caveman trying to start the very first fire ever. Make sure the brush is deep in the sink so you don't spray water all over. Kids ages four and up can be recruited to do this job for you.

For cleaning oil-based products from paintbrushes, substitute paint thinner for water and follow the same procedure. Do this over an empty five-gallon bucket, in an open or well-ventilated area. Wear safety glasses. Cleaning with paint thinner is an adult-only activity.

When working with oil-based products with kids, I love the gelatinous hand cleaners. They feel like squishy, gooey, yucky slime, but they work great to clean oil-based products off of young hands. They come in small cans and are just so dang much fun to use that sometimes I rub them on my torso and run through shopping malls yelling, "Hey, everyone, I've got hand cleaner on my chest!" And when security tries to catch me, they can't because I'm really slippery. Keep this one to yourself. It's really a top-secret tip.

Paint Rollers

For rolling paint, stain, or clear coat polyurethane, the roller of choice for kids is the **14" frame with 1/2" nap roller poly cover,** or "weenie roller," as we like to call them in the trade ($3 to $4).

The roller choice for adults is the **9" professional roller frame with wood handle.** Believe me, after buying cheap roller frames for years under the guise of saving a little money, I can, with all my being, tell you it's just not worth it. The cheap plastic ones suck! Go on, spend the $6. Get the **1/2" cover** for **"all paints,"** as they categorize it ($3.50 to $4.50). The only reason you would need a longer nap roller is if you were painting heavily textured surfaces. And we're not! So don't bother!

Paint Roller Trays

When choosing a **paint roller tray,** I like the rigid, recycled plastic trays. They're easy to clean and they're only a couple of bucks a tray.

Paint Primer

It's a good idea to prime (or base coat) bare wood before you apply the finish coat; this will prevent the wood grain from bleeding through the topcoat of paint. You can get a great **latex/acrylic primer** for $13 to $15 per gallon. I like the latex/acrylic primers for use around kids, because they don't emit toxic fumes. There is nothing worse than having your kid look at you with paint-fume-induced crossed eyes and slur, "Daddy, I see dead people." *All because you decided to use an oil-based paint product.*

Paint

I like to buy **paint** in the $20 to $25 range. Cheap paint requires too many coats to get good coverage on your project. Better quality paint feels thick and rich; like you're applying silky smooth, down-home goodness to everything you paint. Who doesn't want that feeling? Get the better paint! Keep in mind that you can have any color custom mixed for no extra charge. Don't like the colors they have in the store? No problem! Go over to your friend's house and hack off a large chip of the wall color you like. The paint stores have computer mixing machines that can match virtually any color you bring in, so long as your sample is large enough to register—at least the size of a quarter, but no bigger than a hamburger.

The computer can read the color from a picture, a swatch of fabric, a piece of tree bark, a flower, whatever you like. Be creative. It's a lot of fun to say we painted this shelf the color of Grandma's dentures. At least it is for me. Make sure you wash the dentures before you make the paint guy put them under the computer lens.

Painting with water-soluble latex is a kid-appropriate activity from about age seven. Just be sure to lay down plenty of protection for driveways or floors. I suggest outfitting your kid in old clothing, including old shoes.

Polyurethane or Clear Topcoat

Polyurethane is an oil-based product that must be used in a very well-ventilated area. I don't recommend using polyurethane around kids because the fumes are overwhelming. And yet, the finish it produces is extraordinary and difficult to duplicate with **acrylic clear topcoats** (also called polyacrylic). It's also cheaper. But, although it's tempting, unless everyone is in a very well-ventilated area, with can-type respirators on, I say go with the polyacrylic, which doesn't have the problem with fumes and is considered environmentally friendly.

If you do decide to use the oil-based product, keep the kids out of the area until it dries. Polyurethane is $26 to $28 per gallon. The water-based products are $38 to $42 per gallon.

Wood Finish

Most of the projects in this book are designed to be made from wood and will require some type of a finish. Your personal style and home decor will likely dictate the type of finish you want to use. But I will discuss a few of the basic techniques here to give you some ideas. Finishes for wood can range from a simple but elegant wax finish with wood grain showing through, to a more complicated faux paint effect.

Wood stain comes in oil and acrylic bases, just like paint. The choice is yours. If you use an oil-base stain, go with an oil-base clear coat. If you use a water-base stain, go with an acrylic clear coat. Keep in mind that a lot of the acrylic stains require you to use an acrylic clear primer *before* you apply the acrylic stain. Even though acrylic requires a

A Word on the Pre-Finish Steps

Sometimes we get excited and, in a hurry to see our finished product, we skip seemingly irrelevant steps to get to the good part. But I'm here to tell you, *don't rush* . . . and to remind you that *this is not just about the project*, but about spending leisurely, quality family time with your kids and the kids of other neighborhood moms and dads who are not cool enough to get your kids to come over all the time. If you try to rush it, your project won't look as great. And you'll just have to start working on something else. Besides, these steps can make the difference between homemade projects that look homemade and ones that look good enough to seem store-bought, only *cooler*. Take your time. Enjoy the steps.

few more steps, it's definitely worth it if the kids are going to be a part of the finishing process.

Hand-rubbed wax paste, at $12 to $14 per can, is definitely a great option as a finish on any of the pieces you create and build. It looks natural and the kids can help with the application and the steel wool rubdown after the paste wax is applied.

Before you begin, your piece must be well sanded, then waxed, and then rubbed out with some fine grade 0000 steel wool. I've had five-year-olds easily attack every step of the waxing process with no problems.

A Note on Safety with Hand-Rubbed Wax Paste. Paste wax is not something to eat or rub on your siblings! Keep a close eye on the small fry.

PSST . . . WANT A SHORTCUT?

I know you're chomping at the bit to run out, buy some lumber, assemble an array of tools, and posse up your crew. You can't wait to get started on a weekend-long building project that will transform your home into the family-cozy center of the universe you always dreamed it could be. You can only imagine how these projects will ignite the flames of family togetherness and create a lasting memory worthy of its own page in the family scrapbook. *Riiiight!*

I can also envision a blast of reality that finds you, at this very moment, consoling a teething toddler *while* baking a birthday cake *and* preparing for the imminent assault of under-four-foot-tall party guests. You have sixty bucks, three hours, and a tall order for transformation. Because I get that—all too well—wherever possible in these projects, I offer "Shortcut: Under Threes" that allow you to create a similar project in *under three hours* (not including shopping time) and for *under three twenty dollar bills*—or less than $60. Many of these shortcuts will only require a utility knife, some cardboard, a little imagination, and my Do-It-Yourself Family guidance!

2.
The
Kid's
Bedroom

YOUR KID'S BEDROOM is a very important part of the family home. In some ways it might be the most important room in your house because it will function as the command center of your child's early identity and self-esteem. This space is where your son or daughter will start to become autonomous. At first, of course, you'll have brought your new baby home to a room or nursery decorated according to your needs and tastes. But it won't be long before your child is codesigning this room with you. And as time goes on, she will assert her own style through what she collects, how she displays items, and how she ultimately uses her space.

Bedtime is a challenge for most families. Many toddlers resist moving from their crib to a big-kid bed (let alone from *your* bed . . . to a crib . . . to a big-kid bed!). This is why I came up with the Big-Kid-Bed Headboard with Optional Nightlight. Trust me; you're going to love this project as much as your kids will.

BIG-KID-BED HEADBOARD WITH OPTIONAL NIGHTLIGHT

I say the nightlight is optional . . . and it is. However, marrying one of these cool headboards with an easily accessible nightlight is great if your little ones get spooked and need a quick light for nighttime courage, or if they need a dim, cozy glow to make them feel safe all night. This project is so cool I not only can picture you building

Creating a Special Space

When I was a kid, my brother, Kurt, and I used to spend hours designing elaborate shoebox houses for those little troll dolls that were so popular in the seventies. We would wallpaper and paint the cardboard walls, create little troll art mini-paintings and make mini-cardboard furniture. These mini troll dioramas were really fun and very time-consuming. Our obsession with troll dolls provided my parents with an enormous amount of free time.

Designing those troll houses ultimately developed into a greater interest in tricking out our own shoeboxes (aka our bedrooms), prompting us to rearrange our bedrooms and create amazing electrical systems that enabled us to turn our lights and stereo on and off from our beds. Very James Bond. I believe my brother and I enjoyed this deep (but very quiet!) creative play in our rooms because our parents allowed us to have a part in designing them from a very early age. I encourage you to do the same for your children by giving them some free rein over their bedrooms. And, like the lifesaver I am, I'm also here to give you some ideas on how to get started.

it . . . I can actually picture you lying in the new bed, reading this book to your kids.

This simple and easy headboard can be customized or modified as your kids grow and change. This project incorporates the dimensions and designs for a single twin bed, which is the usual first bed for small fry. The standard widths for doubles, queens, kings, and California kings are shown below.

Keep in mind that my suggested designs are merely templates for your own kids' tastes. I encourage you to use your own creativity and experiment! Above all else, have fun and enjoy.

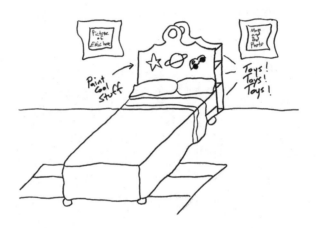

Standard Bed Dimensions

Twin	39" wide x 75" long
Full	54" wide x 75" long
Queen	60" wide x 80" long
King	76" wide x 80" long
King (split)	78" wide x 80" long
California King	72" wide x 84" long

MATERIALS LIST

- 1 sheet of plywood, 3/4" thick
- 1 box of 1½" finishing nails
- Drywall anchors (optional)
- Carpenter's glue
- Primer and paint (see pages 25–26) (I recommend either artist acrylic or semi-gloss latex paint in an array of color choices.)
- Wood dough (hole filler, see page 19)
- Sandpaper (120 and 220 grit, see page 21)
- Paintbrush
- Roller (optional)
- Rope light* (optional)

*Rope lights are an inexpensive string of holiday lights, where the actual lights are encapsulated in a plastic cylinder. They come in varying lengths and colors and produce a nice, soft ambient glow. They don't heat up and they will accommodate a dimmer.

TOOLS

- Circular saw or table saw
- Hammer or nail gun and compressor
- Jigsaw
- Safety glasses
- Tape measure
- Pencil and straightedge or chalk line
- Power drill/screwdriver
- 1/8" drill bit

1. Mark all the cut lines from the diagram onto the 4' x 8' sheet of plywood before you begin to cut. Use a chalk line (see page 17) or pencil lines drawn with a straightedge to get the lines really straight. Accuracy is important here.

Big-Kid-Bed Headboard template

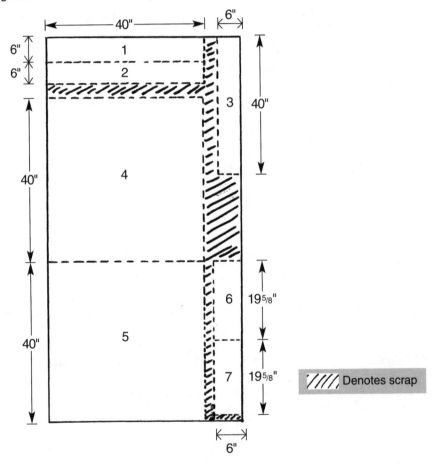

//// Denotes scrap

2. Once all the lines are marked, cut out each piece with a circular saw or table saw. If you wish, you can have the lumberyard cut your pieces for you, for a very nominal fee. You will have seven pieces when finished.

Note: Save or set aside the pieces marked as scrap on the diagram. You will use a small amount of these off-cuts later.

3. Label the seven pieces as follows:

A. Three 40" x 6" pieces, labeled 1, 2, and 3. These will become the center vertical support rail and hidden shelves for toy storage.

B. Two 40" x 40" pieces labeled 4 and 5. These pieces will become the front and back of the headboard.

C. Two 19⅝" x 6" pieces, labeled 6 and 7. These pieces will become the shorter, inner hidden toy storage shelves.

4. Begin by constructing the center support rail and the hidden shelves. Locate pieces 1 and 2. Measure the middle (20" in from one end) and mark with a pencil. Mark piece 2 in the same way.

5. Next, locate piece 3. This is your center support piece. Using your saw, cut 10" from one end, to make the center support 6" x 30". Pieces 1 and 2 will be shelves glued and nailed onto each end of piece 3 on the mark you made in step 4.

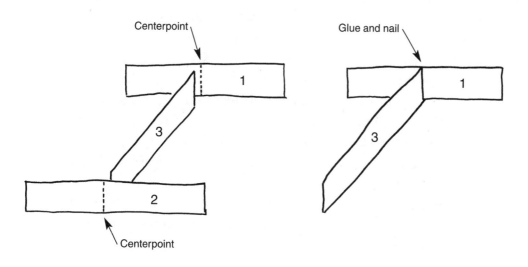

6. From the bottom of the center support (piece 3) measure up 16".
Mark a line in pencil at this point. Next, from the top of the support
measure down 14" and mark this spot in pencil. These marks represent the placement of the shorter, inner shelves (pieces 6 and 7).

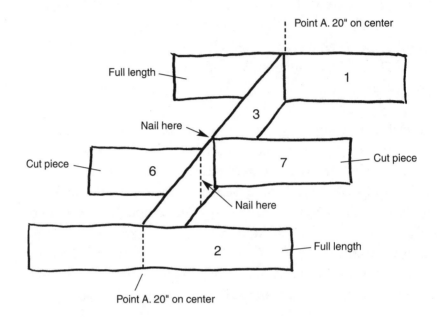

Point A. 20" on center

Full length

1

3

Nail here

Cut piece

6

7

Cut piece

Nail here

2

Full length

Point A. 20" on center

Note: The purpose for this staggered shelf placement is twofold.
One: it's easier to glue and nail the shelves into place, on either side of
the center rail, if their positions are staggered. Two: this means the
shelves will accommodate toys of different sizes. The final construction of the center rail and shelves should resemble this illustration.

7. Locate your scrap wood, cut two pieces at 1" x 16" and two at 1" x
13 1/4". These will be your *story sticks;* they keep your shelving evenly
spaced and parallel while you're nailing the headboard together. They
are only temporary, so don't glue or nail them when assembling your
headboard.

8. Wedge or prop a story stick between each of the shelves to keep
them parallel and evenly spaced. Glue and nail pieces 6 and 7 to the
center support.

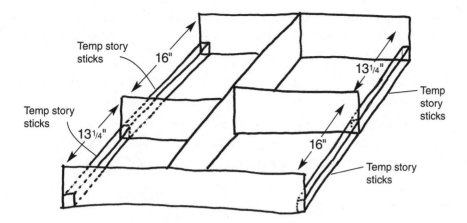

9. Piece 5 will become the front of the headboard. Piece 4 will become the back. You can copy our design as a suggestion, but I suspect that you and your kids will have a lot more fun coming up with your own design together. Once you've unleashed your creativity, use a pencil to sketch the results onto the plywood and cut out with a jigsaw.

CAUTION! Make sure the lowest point of your pattern is $31^{1}/_{2}$" from the bottom of piece 4; otherwise, you will be cutting into the area where your top shelf will be attached.

Stromer Slick Tip: Use a compass or a circular jar to trace the cutout at the top of the headboard. Use the $^{1}/_{8}$" drill bit to create a hole inside the circle. Make the hole large enough to slip in a jigsaw blade. Insert the blade into the hole and begin to carefully cut out your circle.

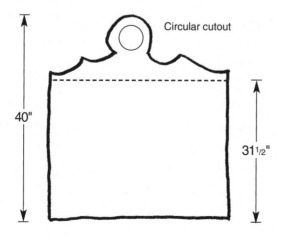

10. Sand any rough edges with 120 and 220 grit sandpaper.

11. Place the cut and sanded piece 4 directly over piece 5 and line up the corners. Use a pencil to trace your incredible design (worthy of a place in a modern art museum) onto piece 5. Set aside piece 4 and repeat your cutting process to create a perfect replica on piece 5.

12. Lay piece 4 on top of the assembled center rail and shelving construction (labeled 1, 2, 3, 6, and 7). Line up the bottom and sides and draw working lines where you will nail down through the plywood into the horizontal edges of the shelves below.

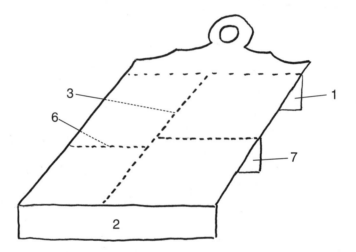

This sounds more difficult than it really is. Once you lay piece 4 on top of the center rail construction, you can look in through the open sides and see where the shelves line up. Use a straightedge and a pencil to draw the line for your nail path.

13. Once you've established the nail path, remove piece 4 and set aside. Run a bead of glue along the top edge of each shelf as well as the center rail.

14. Replace piece 4 on top of this unit, in exactly the same spot, lining up the bottom and sides. Nail straight down into your shelves on the nail line path. Insert one nail every 6". A nail gun will make quick work out of this step. When you are finished, your unit should look like this.

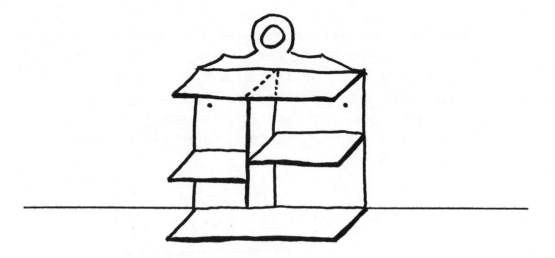

15. Turn the piece over and check along the shelf edges for any glue that may have dripped or oozed out. Wipe it off before it dries in place. Now is a great time to paint the inside of the headboard before you attach the front piece. It is much easier to paint while it's open.

16. After your primer and paint are completely dry, pre-drill a hole on either side of the back of the headboard. The location of these holes is 4" down from the top shelf and 4" in toward the middle from either side as shown. These holes will allow you to secure the headboard to the wall to prevent movement. Personally, I think it's overkill, but if your kids are really rambunctious, it's not a bad idea.

17. If you want to attach the headboard to the wall, move the headboard into its final position and trace the holes onto the wall. Slide the headboard away from the wall; locate your marks on the wall, and screw in your drywall anchors. (See page 18.)

18. Slide the headboard back into place. Prepare two screws, at least 2" long. You want them to be long enough to get through the headboard and into the drywall anchor. Before inserting the screw, thread a washer large enough to keep the head of the screw from going through the hole in the headboard. Tighten the screws just enough to keep the headboard snug against the wall.

Note: To really snug the headboard up against the wall, you may need to remove the baseboard and quarter-round molding. If you do, I recommend that you remove the whole length of baseboard and quarter round, cut out the width of the headboard, and replace the cut pieces on either side. Stash the cutouts in your garage so you can fit it back in place if you change the headboard or room layout.

19. Attach the front headboard piece 5 in exactly the same way you put on the back. Glue and nail.

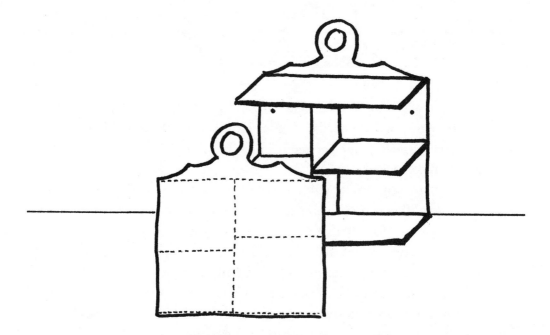

Note: Once the front of the headboard has been installed, you will be able to remove the drywall screws holding the headboard to the wall by using a 3" or shorter (stubby) screwdriver to access the small space.

20. After the front headboard piece is on, fill in all your nail holes and let dry. Then it's time to design and paint all your cool stuff onto the headboard. Make sure you slide your bed up to the headboard so you know which part will be seen. Make a mark and then create your masterpiece above your line.

Paint area
like this

Paint cool
stuff

21. Nightlight options: if you want some light incorporated into your headboard design, the rope light can be easily and safely draped over the top of your headboard or permanently attached by using large U-shaped wire staples, evenly spaced, and by following the silhouette of your super-ultra-fancy Big-Kid-Bed Headboard creation.

22. Slide the bed into place beneath the coolest headboard in three counties, and pass out in *your kid's* bed for a change.

Big-Kid-Bed Headboard with Nightlight Shortcut: Under Threes
The shortcut for the Big-Kid-Bed Headboard is really simple. All you need is a flat, one-half sheet of plywood, cut into a creative shape, painted, and attached to the wall above the bed. The shape and creative design will really add something to your child's big-kid room. The battery-powered, stick-on nightlight is optional.

MATERIALS LIST

 1 half sheet of plywood, 3/4" thick

 1 battery-powered, closet stick-on light (optional)

 Primer

 Paint

 Drywall anchors

TOOLS

Paintbrush

Jigsaw (optional)

Power drill/screwdriver

Safety glasses

Hammer or nail gun and compressor

INSTRUCTIONS

1. To really streamline this shortcut you can have your lumberyard precut the plywood to the width of a twin bed, plus 4", so that it's 43" wide. You will have a piece of plywood 43" x 48". This dimension will easily fit into just about any backseat to transport home.

2. Once home, cut, design, prime, and paint the plywood piece. I couldn't resist sharing four of my favorite beds to give you a few ideas for your own designs. I encourage you to be creative; sketch out any designs or patterns you and your kids agree on. Pre-paint those ideas on the headboard. Go wild. Have fun!

3. Fasten your stick-on light to the plywood. Incorporate it as a design element. Don't be limited by tradition! Any shape is O.K. as long as both you and the kids love it!

4. Pre-drill your headboard at mattress level. Attach to the wall with drywall anchors and slide the bed up to your headboard. The hardest thing about this project is watching the paint dry.

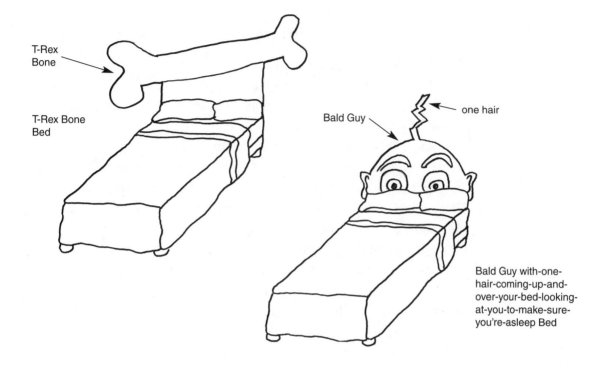

T-Rex Bone

T-Rex Bone Bed

Bald Guy

one hair

Bald Guy with-one-hair-coming-up-and-over-your-bed-looking-at-you-to-make-sure-you're-asleep Bed

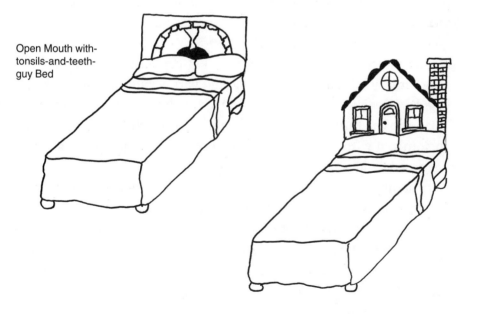

Open Mouth with-tonsils-and-teeth-guy Bed

House with Chimney Bed

UNDER-BED TOY TROLLEY AND GAMEBOARD COMBO

This toy trolley and gameboard combo is one badass concept! It's also a great roll-out building project that reclaims valuable space from dust-bunny land for useful, easy-to-reach storage that both you and your kids will love.

I based this invention on plastic under-bed storage containers. While the store-bought products work well for fixed storage, I've always found them less than ideal for the attention level of children. That's why I call the store-bought products *chaos boxes*. They are great for linens, clothing, and other easily organized dry goods storage, but for toys, *you* can build better!

Here's what I mean: A 7" deep 40" x 20" drawer is about as useful as a pile of toys dumped in the middle of the floor. Whenever my sons, Wyatt and Dusty, pulled these plastic drawers out from under the bed, they would dig through a mass of stuff looking for specific dolls or LEGO pieces. In no time, they would become frustrated and end up dumping everything into the middle of the floor! I had to come in after playtime and pick up what seemed like hundreds of tiny, unrelated toy pieces. As a result, I vowed to create under-bed toy storage that was both efficient and user-friendly!

This project costs just under $50 for two containers and can be built in no time at all. The most complicated part is painting on the gameboard. Your own personal design will dictate how much time you want to spend. The thing I love the most about this project is how it can be customized with drawer inserts to keep all the small game and toy pieces neat and separated.

In addition, I also love that the top keeps out that creepy under-bed fur that seems to permeate everything that lives down there. The cover also serves as a gameboard or train or racetrack for toy trains or cars. Alternatively, it can be painted with a plan or layout view of a play-house . . . a Barbie dance floor . . . or anything your heart—*er*, I mean your *kid's* heart—desires.

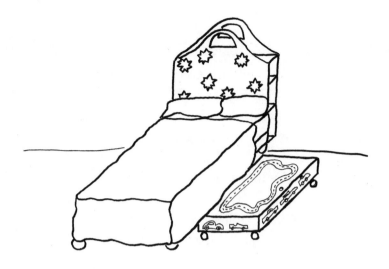

MATERIALS LIST

- 1 sheet of plywood, $1/2$" thick
- Carpenter's glue
- 1 box of $1^1/2$" nails
- Wood dough
- Sandpaper
- Primer
- Paint
- Paintbrush
- 4 small $1^1/2$" casters

TOOLS

- Circular saw or table saw
- Hammer or nail gun and compressor
- Power drill/screwdriver
- Safety glasses
- Pencil and straightedge or chalk line
- Tape measure

Note: One sheet of plywood will make two 36" x 20" under-bed trolleys.

Use a chalk line (see page 17), or a pencil and straightedge to draw the cut lines onto the full sheet of plywood.

1. Once your sheet of plywood is carefully measured and marked, you can cut out each piece with your table saw or circular saw. You will have 26 pieces.

2. Label each piece with a pencil as shown.

A. 4 pieces 20" x 36", labeled 1 through 4. These pieces are the tops and bottoms of the trolley.

B. 4 pieces 5" x 20", labeled 5 through 8. These pieces are the short sides.

C. 2 pieces 4 1/2" x 20", labeled 9 and 10. These pieces are the dividers.

D. 4 pieces 5" x 37", labeled 11 through 14. These pieces are the long sides.

E. 12 pieces 1" x 6", labeled 15 through 22. These pieces are spacers.

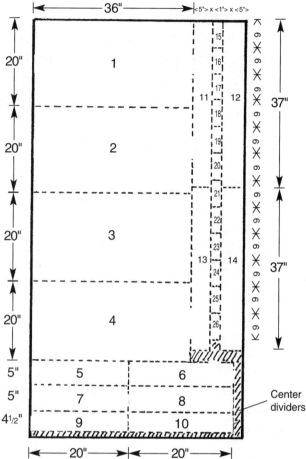

Under-Bed Trolley plywood template cutout

36"

<5"> x <1"> x <5">

20"

20"

20"

20"

5"

5"

4½"

37"

37"

1

2

3

4

5

6

7

8

9

10

11

12

13

14

15

16

17

18

19

20

21

22

23

24

25

26

20"

20"

Center dividers

Denotes scrap

Note: Since you're building two boxes, separate your pieces as follows: pieces 1, 2, 5, 6, 9, 11, 12, 15, 16, 17, 18, 19, and 20 are for box one. Set aside pieces 3, 4, 7, 8, 10, 13, 14, 21, 22, 23, 24, 25, and 26 for the second box.

3. The under-bed trolley is essentially a 37" x 20" box on wheels, with dividers and a lid. To build the first box, take piece 1 (the bottom) and glue and nail pieces 11 and 12 onto each 36" side.

Note: Pieces 11 and 12 are 1" longer than piece 1. This will enable you to center pieces 11 and 12 along the length of piece 1 so that ½" hangs off each end. This overhang will allow the short pieces (numbers 5 and 6) a perfect flush corner fit.

4. Next locate pieces 5 and 6. These are the short-end pieces to your box. Apply glue to the edge of the bottom and the side edges where the corners join to insure a strong bond. Fit the pieces in place and nail securely every 6". You should now have a 5" deep trolley tray.

Under-Bed Trolley assembly

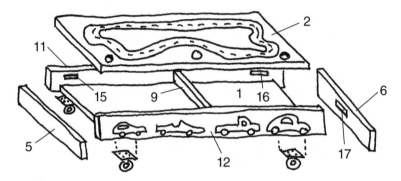

5. If you wish to insert a divider, find the center along the 36" sides and mark it at 18". Draw a line across the trolley bottom and glue the divider (piece 9) to the bottom. Turn the piece over and nail from underneath. You may want to put a nail through each side of the trolley to really make sure the divider stays in place.

Glue and nail supports for inset lid

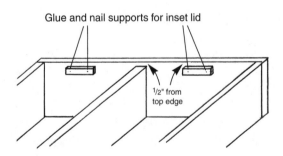

1/2" from top edge

6. Locate support pieces (15 through 20 for box 1 and 21 through 26 for box 2) and glue and nail onto the inside edge of the trolley, 1/2" down from the top edge and 2" in from all four corners on the 36" side. These pieces will enable the trolley lid to be inset and sit flush with the top edge of the toy trolley.

7. Drill two 1/2" holes on the front edge of the lid, at both the right and left corners. This will be your finger-pull to easily open the lid. Sand the inside of these holes smooth.

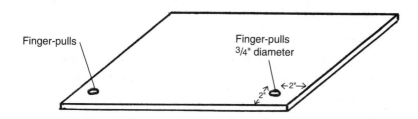

Finger-pulls

Finger-pulls
3/4" diameter

8. Install the casters on the bottom of the trolley 1" in from all corners. When installing casters, mark their positions and screw holes with a pencil, then remove the caster and pre-drill. You want to make a pilot hole using a smaller drill bit than the size of the caster screw. Make sure you don't drill all the way through the 1/2" base of the trolley floor. Position the casters over the pre-drilled holes and screw them in.

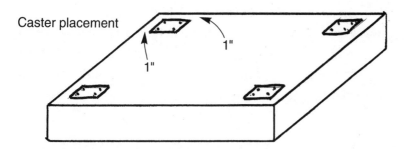

Caster placement

1"

1"

Stromer Slick Tip: To keep from drilling too deep into wood, I like to wrap a piece of tape slightly less than 1/2" up from the tip of the drill bit to give me an accurate depth gauge. For an illustration, see page 129.

9. Fill all nail holes with wood dough, sand any rough spots, and prime every surface. Run your hands over the surfaces after you have primed and patched all the holes. You want the edges to feel completely smooth and finished.

10. Prime the lid and set aside until you have finished painting the base.

11. After you have made some sketches on paper for the design of your top trolley art, transfer the sketches onto the top in pencil. Once you are satisfied with your design, retrace over your existing pencil lines with an indelible marker.

12. Take out your artist's brushes and fill in between your lines with color. Feel free to use latex craft paint or even colored, indelible markers. If you accidentally get paint on your lines, don't worry; you can always retrace the lines with the marker.

13. After the paint is dry, load your trolley up with toys and slide it under your bed until you want to play. Have fun, you nutty little organizer!

14. Now go on to complete box two . . . you know you want to.

Under-Bed Trolley Shortcut: Under Threes Go ahead and buy the plastic or laminated under-bed storage. It's a little pricey and not as easy to customize, but I get it that you need some order in your life and in your kids' room . . . and you need it *now*. Getting organized is the priority. You can always come back and build these later.

If you want to decorate the top of the plastic boxes, be creative. You can even make it a gameboard. I recommend that you use craft paint products specially formulated for painting on plastic. Craft stores have primer and sealant for this purpose.

INCREDIBLE TOTABLE RECREATION STATION

This amazing project is like a portable briefcase for toys. It gives you and your kids a way to create and contain a little adventure land, much like I did with my shoebox troll houses.

The Incredible Totable Recreation Station can be a minihouse, barn, condo, casino (did I just write that?), or whatever you like. For our purposes, I'll show you how to create a cool little fantasy house for play figures your kids may already have or can create. This project has a cool exterior that acts as a carrying case that also holds all the required play pieces.

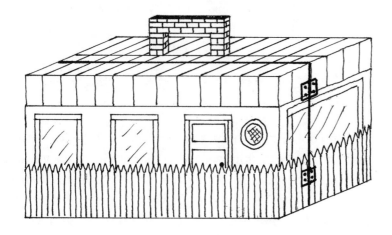

Here are some examples of mini furniture you can create.

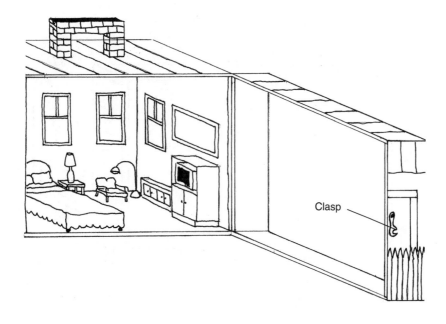

Clasp

These are some of my favorite Stromer family characters.

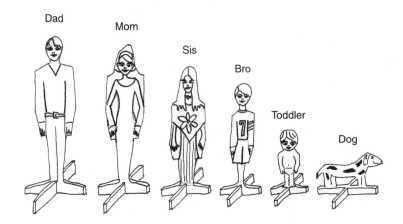

The other cool thing about the Incredible Totable Recreation Station is that it can be customized to suit boy or girl characters and individual design preferences. It's a great way to remodel their room with very little cost to Mom and Dad. My kids spend hours playing with this house. And best of all, they can take it with them when they go to Grandma and Grandpa's. . . .

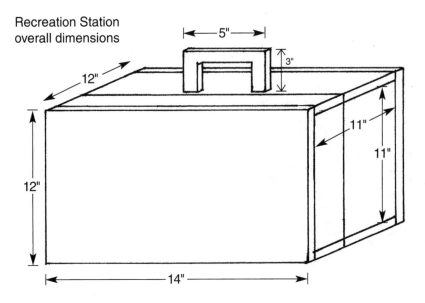

- 1 half sheet of plywood, ½" thick (makes *two* recreation stations)
- 1 box of 1¼" nails
- 1 small clasp to close your recreation station for transport
- 2 small hinges
- 1 drawer pull with handle styling
- Primer and latex semi-gloss or acrylic artist craft paint (choose your colors!)
- Carpenter's glue
- Indelible black marker
- Ten 1" wood screws

TOOLS

- Circular saw or table saw
- Hammer or nail gun and compressor
- Power drill/screwdriver
- Paintbrush (2½" is my favorite size)
- Artist paintbrush (small enough to paint with control between ½" lines)
- Pencil and straightedge or chalk line (optional)
- Tape measure
- Safety glasses

1. Transfer the entire template onto the sheet of plywood before you begin to make your cuts. Cut carefully, using your circular saw or table saw. Or, if you wish, you can have the cuts made at your lumber store. (You will have 12 usable pieces.)

Recreation Station template

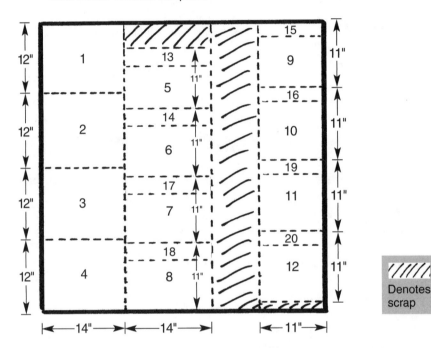

2. Label the pieces 1 through 20 as shown.

A. 4 pieces 12" x 14", labeled 1 through 4. These pieces are the full-size, outside pieces for the two boxes.

B. 4 pieces 11" x 14", labeled 5 through 8. These pieces are the top and bottom for two boxes.

C. 4 pieces 11" x 11", labeled 9 through 12. These are the end pieces for the two boxes.

3. Crosscut pieces 5 and 6 as shown below. This will give you additional pieces. Label them as 13 and 14. These pieces will create the top and bottom of both the deep and shallow sides of the box. (For box two, repeat these instructions with pieces 7 and 8. Label the new pieces 17 and 18.)

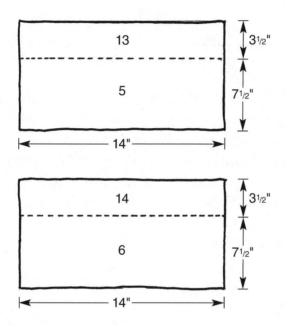

4. Crosscut pieces 9 and 10 as shown. This will give you additional pieces. Label them as 15 and 16. They will create the ends of both the deep and shallow sides of the box as shown on the next page. (For box two, repeat these instructions with pieces 11 and 12. Label the new pieces 19 and 20.)

Note: Pieces 1, 2, 5, 6, 9, 10, and 13 through 16 construct box one. Set aside pieces 3, 4, 7, 8, 11, 12, and 17 through 20 to construct box two.

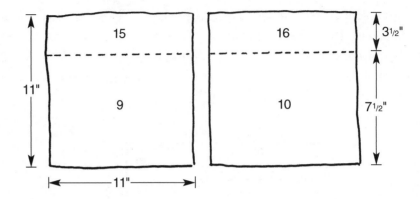

5. Next, assemble the shallow side of the box. First glue and then nail the long pieces, 13 and 14, to piece 1. Pieces 13 and 14 will line up evenly with the long edges of piece 1. The shorter-end pieces 15 and 16, insert between 13 and 14 to complete a flush edge all the way around. Don't forget to apply a thin bead of glue to the corner edges before you insert them to insure the strength and support your box lid requires.

Recreation Station shallow side

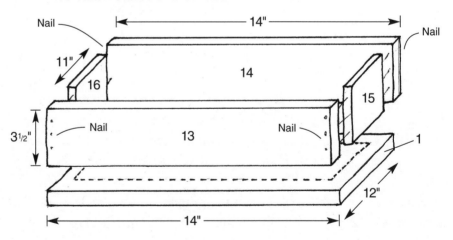

6. The next step is to create the deep side of the box by repeating the same process shown in step 5. The base begins with full-size piece 2, to which you will attach pieces 5, 6, 9, and 10, as we did in step 5.

You should now have two rectangular open-sided boxes, one deep and one shallow.

Recreation Station deep side

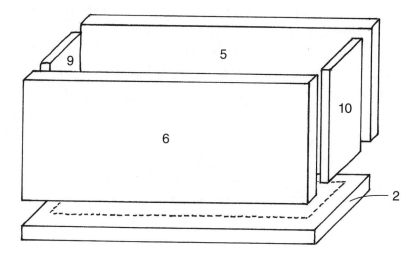

When put together, these boxes should have an overall dimension of 14" x 12".

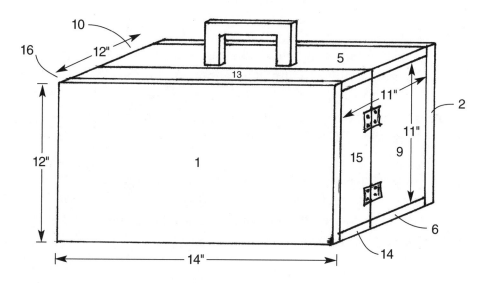

7. Attach the hinges 1" from the top and bottom of your recreation station on the right side of the box where the two pieces meet.

8. On the left side, fasten your clasp system dead center from the top and bottom of your recreation station where the two pieces meet. This will give you the ability to lock up and transport your recreation station without losing the contents of your playhouse. See the drawings of mini furniture on page 51 for clasp style and placement.

9. Attach the drawer pull right at 6" on center along the top of your recreation station.

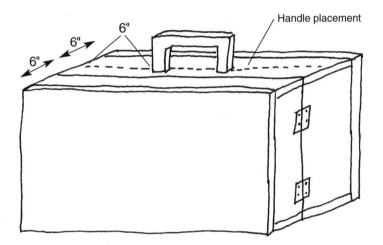

10. Now you are ready to sand it smooth and prime. Brush on primer, being careful not to hit the hinges or clasp.

Stromer Slick Tip: Use a cotton swab to apply a small amount of petroleum jelly to the hinges and clasp to protect them from the paint.

11. Let dry and sketch out your artwork. This is where your creativity can really come alive. Draw on windows, fences, flowers, curtains, you name it! After you are satisfied with your design, go ahead and trace over what you like with an indelible marker.

12. Use your artist's brush and colorful craft paint to carefully paint between the lines and watch your Totable Recreation Station come alive!

13. Furniture can be created with anything you can find. A thread spool and a piece of cardboard cut in a circle and glued on top make a great table. Blue-tip matchboxes can become great trundle beds when stuffed with tissue bedding. Coffee stirrers can be glued together to create great chairs, tables, picture frames, etc. Did I mention buttons, beads, pasta, baby food jar lids, pinecone Christmas trees, spice bottle tops, and butter stick cardboard boxes to create a refrigerator or shower stall? There is a world of recreation station furniture possibilities awaiting your discovery. So get busy looking!

I have also included simple traceable figures that you can create by filling in the silhouettes. These figures can be enhanced by your artistry. You can create your own family by tracing the characters in the Stromer family on page 52.

Stromer Family Cutouts:

1. Lay out your 1/2" thick scrap plywood and copy these guys onto your wood.

2. Slowly cut out your pieces and lightly sand the edges.

3. Cut a 1/4" x 1/4" parallel groove up into the base of the characters.

4. Cut a 1/4" x 11/2" strip of plywood.

5. Glue the 1/4" x 11/2" piece in a cross in the groove.

6. Pencil in your characters, then highlight with an indelible marker.

7. Fill in with paint, colored pencil, or marker.

8. Play like you've never played before!

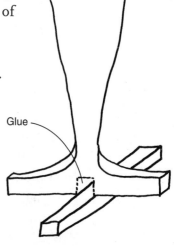

Glue

Rotating Art Wall Shortcut for Recreation Station: Under Threes The Totable Recreation Station is all about fostering our children's creativity. But the truth is, fostering creativity is something you can do without building a thing. Most of us decorate our children's rooms by hanging pictures and posters at eye level . . . *adult eye level*! It might look good to you, but think about the little guys. Pictures at our height are meaningless to them.

Thanks to my dad, an art dealer, I spent years watching how art is mounted for exhibition, and decided that the **Rotating Art Wall** would be a great way to encourage my kids to produce quick and easy art in their own rooms.

The Rotating Art Wall is best when set up in a corner, but any wall

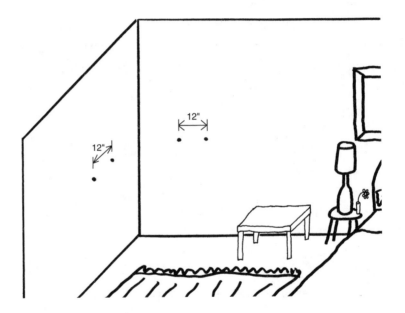

space will do. Simply purchase a combination of art boards: chalkboard, whiteboard, corkboard, and magnetic bulletin boards. Hang a combination of two or more boards, low enough to allow your mini van Goghs to write, draw, and create at will. Vary the texture and medium. Pair a chalkboard on the left wall with a corkboard on the right wall. Or, match up a whiteboard with a magnetic bulletin board.

The cool thing about this project is that there is no setup necessary to get your kids started. When they want to paint or create chalk drawings, a canvas is ready to go. One day they can choose chalk . . . tomorrow you can rotate the boards and let them play with magnets and dry-erase markers. They can even paint, using a corkboard and some tacks as an easy easel that won't tip over.

Don't forget, like many of my favorite projects in this book, this simple-to-create art wall can just as easily be broken down for storage in seconds.

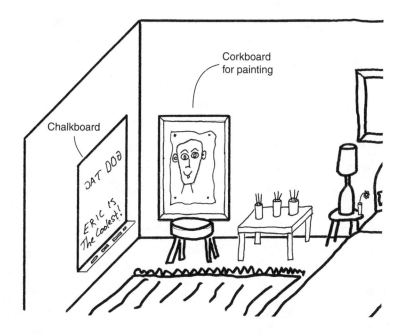

Stromer Slick Tip: For these in-bedroom art project areas I purchased one of those plastic mats used under rolling desk chairs in carpeted offices. I put that on the floor below the corkboard easel. I tell my kids, "Try to keep the paint on the paper, but if it drips, it's O.K. because you're on the mat." Remind them to wipe their shoes off before they step from the mat onto carpet or flooring. Having an old towel nearby for this purpose will help them remember.

I have spent a lifetime trying to figure out how to easily clean up, organize, and store toys for my kids (O.K., maybe not a *lifetime*, but it sure seems that way). I have also tried to understand *why* kids don't just store toys themselves. I mean, if they can take them out . . . right?

To learn more about this perplexing phenomenon, I observed my kids at play while making notes on my scientific-looking clipboard. By the way, I look great in a lab coat, but then again, who doesn't? And what I found, after they looked at me and said, "Quit looking at us in that creepy lab coat," was that we hadn't established storage places that we all—meaning, Amy, me, *and* our kids—agreed upon. My systems were random and mine—they were *not* systems *created by my kids*. In other words, until I got an "I get it" sign-on from my boys, any feeble attempts at order would be met with blank stares. How were my kids supposed to know what to do with their toys if I didn't even know? So my older son and I decided to sit down together and create a system that we both understood.

Here's what we came up with:

1. **Dolls and action figures.** These become a tangled mess when deposited en masse in a drawer. To find one you feel like playing with, you have to pull them all out. *Alert*: instant pile of dolls on the floor. I solved this with an old shoe-hanging organizer—the kind with pouches—meant to be hung on the back of a door. Tuck a doll or two into each pouch and it's like they each have their own little shoe pouch condo for themselves and perhaps a roommate or two.

2. **Everything else goes in marked shoeboxes.** When you buy your kids shoes, which, let's face it, you seem to do every five minutes, save the boxes. Take an instant or digital photo of the type of toy that will be in the box and tape it to the outside end of the box; for example, toy cars, art supplies, dolls. Stack the boxes on the floor or on the top shelf of the closet. What's inside will be easy to spot based on the photos.

3. **Keep instructions forever.** How many times have you bought one of those expensive LEGO assembly-required boxes with all the little pieces and, after the first assembly, you lose the one piece that holds it all together? It becomes a onetime toy because the directions get lost and the pieces get thrown in a toy drawer—casualties of the *toy box chaos*! Next time you are in this predicament, tear off the front page of the directions, which shows the completed project, tape it to a coffee can, paint can, or empty diaper wipe container, and put all the pieces inside with the rest of the directions.

4. **Art supplies.** I love the look of art supplies. Crayons, color pens, paintbrushes, colored markers—the different colors and textures of these items look great stored in clear containers. Organize these supplies so that they become a part of your room decor. Collect them all and put them in empty pickle, mayo, or applesauce jars, or any see-through plastic container for stacking on a shelf. They can become a great display feature in any room, while creating order and providing easy access.

5. **Display art.** Place a 1" x 6" shelf, 12" from the ceiling, all the way around the perimeter of your kids' room. That area of the wall is always underutilized and offers great display accommodations for stuffed animals, dolls, trophies, photos, or just about anything with great display value. In an average 10' x 12' room, that's 44 linear feet of shelving!

3.
The
Master
Bedroom

THE MASTER BEDROOM *should* be a sanctuary from the hassles and stress of everyday life. In real life, that's not always the case. You start your relationship with the bedroom serving as a place for romance, intimacy, and rest. Pretty soon, as a direct consequence of all that romance, kids show up. Almost immediately, exhaustion overcomes you and it seems easier and more efficient to allow some of the kid monkey business to spill over into your once-private sanctuary. The result? *There goes the master bedroom!*

Another challenge for happy master bedroom living is a lack of closet space, or inefficient use of closet space. Why? Simple:

because you sleep there, your kids seem to drag all their junk in there as well. Clutter becomes a large issue. TVs, videotapes, DVDs, magazines, clothes, and books can rage out of control fast; without efficient storage solutions, your *bed*room becomes the *dread* room.

Finally—and perhaps more important—do you remember that guy or girl you married several years ago? You know, the one you used to go out with on dinner dates and stuff . . . before all those toys and kids separated you from your spouse . . . in your *own bed*? That's right, I said it! Romance! It all starts by reclaiming your space before it's too late!

HIS AND HER CLOSETS

His closet and her closet have drastically different needs. Her closet needs a tremendous amount of short and long hanging space. Shoes and purses can become a real issue. And if you don't have a dresser in your room, drawers in the closet are essential. If you are the Imelda Marcos type when it comes to shoes, I suggest you rent a condo for shoe storage and we'll call it a day. If you are like most of us, the closet you do have is probably sufficient once you make the most of what you have. *Don't roll your eyes!* I've got a plan for maximizing your existing closet space.

His closet can have the same configuration but will probably have to house all of her leftover hanging stuff that she doesn't want to get rid of.

In my opinion, the traditional horizontal pole and top shelf is a waste of precious closet space. That space above the top shelf is generally stacked with purses and boxes that give you the same access to your stuff as an old attic you require a stepladder to peer into. There is probably at least 30 cubic feet of perfectly good space that can be utilized if you just reconfigure it slightly. 'Nuff said.

Here is an example of the standard closet configuration. Notice all the wasted space at the top and bottom.

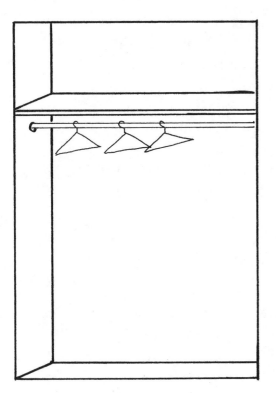

On the left is a typical closet configuration which might look a lot like yours. On the right is that same closet with a little reconfiguration. I try to maximize every little part of it. Same closet, with substantially more usable space! The prefab closet kits are limited in size varieties. I'm here to show you how to have the closet of your dreams with maximum functionality.

MATERIALS LIST

 1 sheet of plywood, 3/4" thick

 1 box of 1½" drywall anchors, or 1½" nails for your shiny new nail gun and compressor

 1 wooden closet pole with attachment hardware

 Carpenter's glue

 1 vial of antidepressants to get you through the first week without the clothes you thought you couldn't live without

 Enough wooden hangers to rehang what clothes you have left

TOOLS

 Circular saw or table saw

 Hammer or nail gun and compressor

Safety glasses

Power drill/screwdriver

Tape measure

 Level

 Pencil and straightedge or chalk line

 ½-ton pickup to haul away all the clothes you'll never wear again

Note: The standard closet width is 48". Taking that into consideration, the materials for this design are gauged for the standard closet width.

1. Use your table or circular saw to cut the sheet of plywood into four 12" x 8' lengths. Two of the lengths will create the closet organizer; set aside the other two for facing.

2. Tear out the existing closet pole configuration. Notice how there is a 1" x 2" piece of wood holding up your closet shelf. You will utilize this method to hang your new shelving.

3. Measure the full width of your closet and cut one of your 1' x 8' shelves to fit that width.

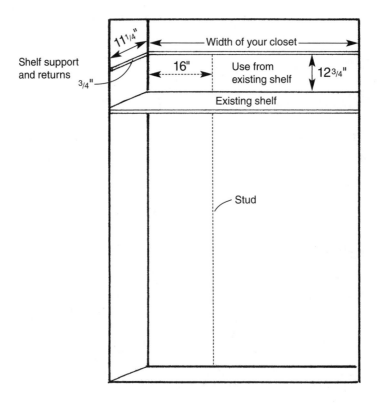

4. From one of your remaining 8' lengths, cut two strips 1 1/2" wide, which will face your entire closet.

5. Cut another piece the same width as your shelf to 3/4" wide.

6. From the remaining piece, cut one more piece 3/4" x 22¹/2", then cut that in half to make two 11¹/4" pieces. These will become the shelf return pieces.

7. Measure up from your existing shelf 12³/4" and, with a level, draw a line around the perimeter of your closet. Bring that line along the side walls, as well.

8. Line up the 3/4" support piece on the line that you made. Nail into both corners first.

Note: You will always find a stud in the corners of your closet, which gives added support to your shelf installation. Measure out 16" from the corners toward the center of your closet and you should find more wood to nail into. If you don't, use a stud finder or tap a 3" nail along the line every inch until you hit solid wood. Make a mark with a pencil and nail your 3/4" piece on your mark. Don't worry about patching because your shelf will hide the holes you have made.

9. Nail in your side support pieces. If you have trouble finding wood, pre-drill a hole at either end of your 3/4" x 11¹/4" piece while holding it to the drywall. Remove the piece and drill in two wall anchors in the spot where your drill bit went into the drywall. Screw in the accompanying screw through your piece and into the drywall anchor. See page 18 for information on wall anchors. Repeat on the other side.

10. Lay your shelf on top of the support pieces, and nail down into them. Use two nails on each side and three nails in the back all evenly spaced.

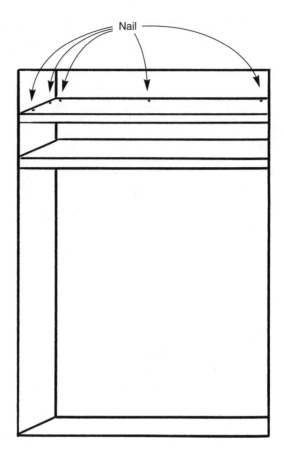

11. Glue the facing onto the front of your shelf and put your 1¹/₂"
piece of facing flush with the top of the shelf and nail into the face
edge of your plywood. Nail every 8", evenly spaced.

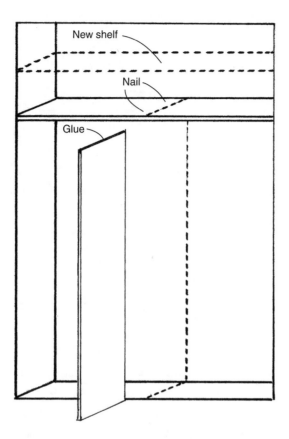

New shelf

Nail

Glue

Congratulations, you have now mastered the fine art of rigid span shelf-making. By using the 1¹/₂" piece of facing you have now made your shelf sag proof!

12. From your existing shelf, measure exactly the center point of your closet and make a mark on the face of that shelf.

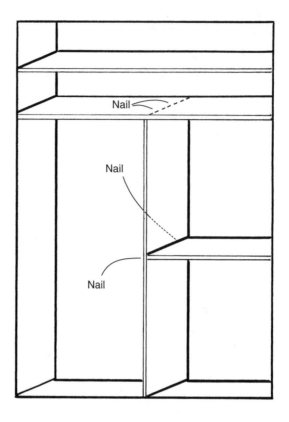

Nail

Nail

Nail

13. Measure from the bottom of that shelf to the floor and write that number down. Grab another piece of 1' x 8' shelving stock and cut it to your desired length.

14. Bring it to your closet, glue the top edge, and slide it right under your centerpoint line. Nail down through the top of the shelf and into your vertical divider piece. (Refer to the illustration for step 11.) Use your level and make sure that piece is plumb. Remember that "plumb" means that when you hold the level to the vertical piece, the bubble is right in the center between the lines. For more information on using a level, see page 17.

15. Now measure the distance between the vertical divider and the wall to the right. Cut one more shelf to that width.

16. Measure the distance from the bottom of your existing shelf to the floor. Divide this space in half, and mark a line on all three sides, including the vertical divider.

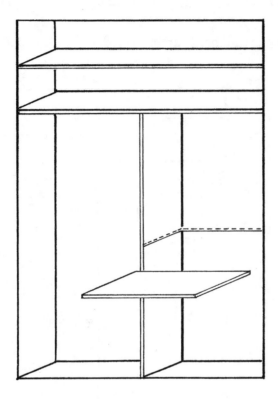

17. Cut shelf support pieces as follows: two return pieces to 3/4" x 11 1/4", and one shelf support piece to the width of your closet in that space x 3/4".

18. Install the back support piece first, and nail in place. Then fit in the side support pieces on the sides. Make sure they are level or your shelf won't fit properly.

19. Lay in your shelf, and nail it down.

20. Grab some of your shirts or blouses, and hold them below your two shelves on the right side of your closet to a position where they

don't touch the ground. Preferably higher so they allow stacked shoe-boxes or shoes below.

21. Measure down from your shelves to find level and hang your closet pole below the facing, leaving enough room so that your hangers will clear the pole.

22. Attach with the hardware provided and cut the pole to length.

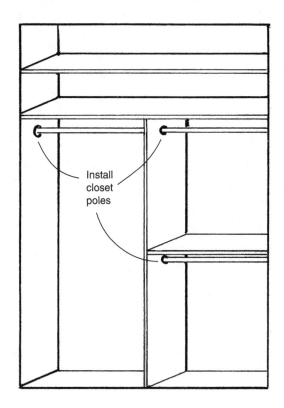

Install closet poles

23. Hold up your longest clothing in the left side of the closet and make a mark. Again, measure down from the upper shelf to find level.

24. Cut the pole to length and install with the hardware provided.

25. With your remaining plywood, rip $1^1/2$" strips that you will center on all exposed edges to match your upper shelf. This gives the closet system a built-in look.

26. You now have way more efficient space and 30% to 50% more usable volume. Now, don't fill it up or I'll come after you with a water bottle!

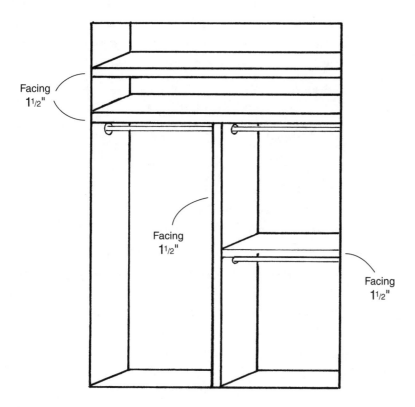

Facing
1½"

Facing
1½"

Facing
1½"

His and Her Closets Shortcut: Under Threes If this closet system seems too complicated, then let's just work with what you already have. After several years working on TLC's *Clean Sweep* television program, I observed hundreds of people parting with clutter and, in some cases, hoarding possessions for no other reason than their unwillingness to let go of the past.

Some of the most emotional stories involved people who finally made the decision to let go of old clothing, collectibles, toys, and various unused personal belongings. No joke; I saw grown men and women cry as we carted away old clothes that no longer fit or were long out of style.

Some of the attachment to old clothing was related to a desire to lose weight and the hope that one day they would be able to fit back into their high school chinos, skinny jeans, or college graduation dress. But, as a guy who only parted with his "college pants" last year, I discovered that when my desired weight did come off, I no longer wanted to wear a pair of woefully out-of-date jeans that reeked of patchouli oil. Who wants to look and smell like a walking Grateful Dead concert, anyway?

Now, about that purple Nehru jacket . . . get rid of it! This is the single most important thing you can do to make room for the new, far-more-organized life you've been fantasizing about!

After you have purged your past of embarrassing fashions from the seventies and eighties, throw out all your wire hangers. Then you must purchase (*cue the sound of angels singing*) wooden hangers.

Wooden hangers actually *prevent* you from accumulating too many clothes. You can't pack or force clothing into your closet like a sardine can if you have wooden hangers. They are the great restriction when it comes to introducing new clothing into your closet. It's almost like rushing a sorority with wooden hangers, all the other clothes have to make sure you "fit in," or you are unmercifully crucified and blackballed at the next gathering! If the clothes don't fit, you must submit to the idea that for every new item you purchase, you must get rid of something you don't wear from last season! And, no, I'm not kidding. Or crazy. Really.

For shoes: keep the boxes and take pictures of the shoes in profile, then tape the photos to the box. They can be stacked on the newly improved and vastly more practical upper shelf for easy access and return. That frees up your floor space for low plastic containers housing sweaters, purses and other bulky items, or more stacked shoeboxes.

HANG-UPS: THE GOOD KIND—
INCREDIBLE HOOK AND MIRROR COMBO UNIT

Don't forget the often-overlooked back of the door for hanging shoes, purses, and robes or (in my perfect universe) for tool storage. This is an ideal way to maximize an empty space with a practical solution.

Hang-ups are a quick and easy way to keep clothes, purses, hats, and towels off the floor and bed. With a few simple hooks or shelving systems, you can keep the master bedroom clutter-free.

Why is this cool?

Three words: STUFF . . . OFF . . . FLOOR!

Hook, hooks, hooks, I tell you! They're all the rage for the new millennium. You need 'em, and here's why: according to the International Hook Institute's controversial study from Stuttgart, Germany (June 2004), it was determined that "irrefutable evidence suggests that hooks and other hanging devices have saved more marriages due to the removal of floor debris (clothing), than any other factor to date!" Clear the bed . . . clear the floor . . . clear your mind . . . and the rest will follow!

This controversial study compelled me to design my Incredible Hook and Mirror Combo Unit. It can be used as a catchall for anything that needs to be hung. It looks cool and the mirror gives you, the person doing the responsible hanging, a chance to wink at yourself as you hang that pair of jeans formerly on the floor, and say, "Hey, you! Foxy little hanger, you just saved your marriage again! And, darn it, you're good-looking."

Hang-ups

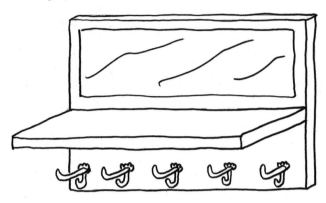

MATERIALS LIST

- One 1' x 3' mirror
- Mirror adhesive
- Mirror hardware to attach to frame (optional)
- 1 half sheet of plywood, ¾" thick

- 4 or 5 decorative hooks of your choice with mounting screws
- Paint, stain, or clear coat finish
- One 1" x 4" x 8' pine board

TOOLS

- Circular saw or table saw
- Power drill/screwdriver
- Safety glasses
- Tape measure

- Pencil and straightedge or chalk line
- Level for hanging

1. Take your 4' x 4' piece of plywood, and rip 6" off of one side, using your circular or table saw.

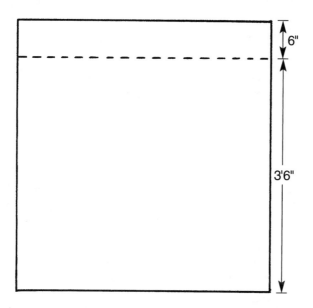

2. The piece you cut off will become the shelf. Make a mark 7 1/4" from the bottom, along the full 4' run of the wood.

3. Glue the back of the 6" cut piece and place it on the line.

4. Nail from the back into your new shelf.

5. Locate your 1' x 4' pine board and cut three strips 3/4" wide from the full 8' length. Then, from two strips, cut one 42" long and one strip 49 1/2". These strips will become the facing around the outside of your mirror and hook combo. From the final strip, cut one strip 49 1/2" long and two strips 6" long. This will be the facing on your shelf.

6. Glue the side edge and place your 42" piece flush with the top and the bottom.

7. Nail four evenly spaced nails.

8. Repeat on the other side.

9. Repeat on the top and bottom.

10. Equally space your hooks below your shelf and screw them evenly across the span of the 4' run.

11. Lay your piece flat and position your mirror where you like it. I prefer it centered between the top of the shelf and the top edge of the piece.

12. Trace around the mirror and remove.

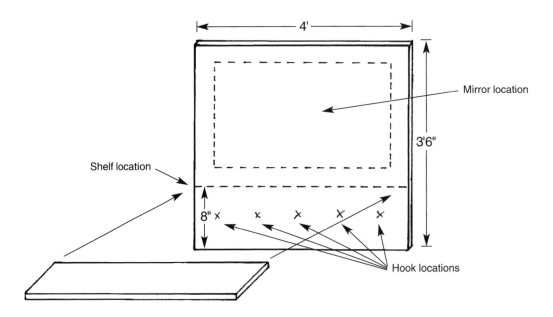

13. Place adhesive on the plywood and gently press the mirror into place. Let adhesive dry according to manufacturer's recommendation. The adhesive might be enough to keep the mirror in place permanently; however, installation of mirror hardware along the edges will give you extra peace of mind and a more finished look.

14. Prime and paint or stain and clear coat.

15. Hang my amazing marriage saver on the wall and thank me later.

BED WITH WINGS

It's 2 A.M. and one (or more) of your kids is sick or scared. He wants to sleep in your bed . . . with his stuffed bear . . . and the dog . . . and Mr. Timmins (my son's imaginary friend). Will you get any sleep among all those arms and legs and kicking and scratching?

Of course you will. The Bed with Wings allows children, teddy, Mr. Timmins, and the pets to sleep close by on roll-out mattresses that work with any bed that has room for under-bed storage.

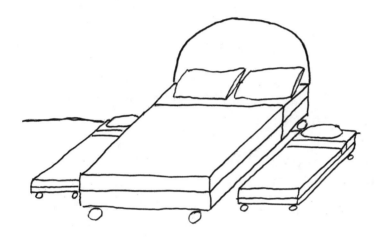

MATERIALS LIST	
1 sheet of plywood, 3/4" thick (makes two)	Wood dough
Carpenter's glue	Sandpaper (120 and 220 grit)
1 box of 1½" nails	4 handles (makes two)
10 small casters (1½" to 2" tall) (makes two)	Two 20" x 36" sections of 4" thick foam (makes two)
Primer and paint	

- Circular saw or table saw
- Hammer or nail gun and compressor
- Power drill/screwdriver
- Safety glasses
- Pencil and straightedge or chalk line
- Tape measure
- Paintbrush and roller

INSTRUCTIONS

1. Transfer the diagrams to your plywood and cut out the pieces as shown. You should end up with the following 12 pieces, labeled with numbers as shown on the diagram.

    A. 4 pieces 20" x 36" labeled 1 through 4.

    B. 4 pieces 5" x 20" labeled 5 through 8.

    C. 4 pieces 5" x 37½" labeled 9 through 12.

Bed with Wings template

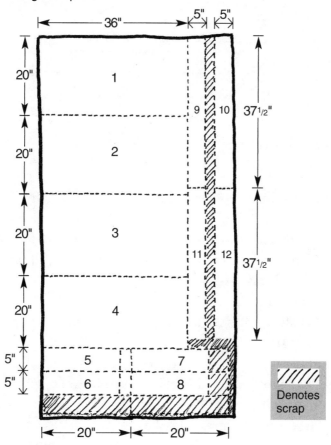

2. Take piece 1 (the bottom) and first glue and nail the long sides, pieces 9 and 10, into place. Note that you want to center the long pieces so that 3/4" hangs off on each end.

3. Next, attach the two short side pieces, numbers 5 and 6, to complete the sides of the bed tray. Notice how they inset into that overhang space and line up flush with the bottom and sides. Make sure you nail the corners to each other, and don't forget glue where the corners meet.

Bed with Wings assembly

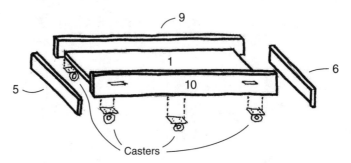

4. Repeat for the other bed tray using the remaining pieces (numbers 2, 7, 8, 11, and 12).

5. Flip the bed trays over and screw in five casters to each bottom. Inset each caster 1" from the corners. Place the fifth caster in the center of the bed tray.

6. Prime and paint.

7. Install handles on the front of piece 10, 4" from each end, and 2½" down from top.

8. Place the pre-cut 20" x 36" piece of foam in each of the bed trays.

9. Put a small sheet, a blanket, and an extra pillow on the bed and roll under your bed on both sides if you have two children.

10. If you only have one, use the extra bed tray as a soapbox derby car!

11. Store your extra two 20" x 36" pieces (numbers 3 and 4) in the garage for future under-bed storage lids. Or cut them in half and use the extra wood as garage or household shelving.

This Bed with Wings project reunited me with the woman I married. I had forgotten how beautiful she looked when she slept because I hadn't seen her in seven years! We were so afraid that we would someday have to have the following conversation with our boys unless I figured out how to remedy this with the Bed with Wings project.

MASTER BEDROOM—NIGHT: *Four grown adults sleeping uncomfortably in a fetid, cluttered room. An old, scared man in his sixties and his gray-haired wife, the same age but still radiantly beautiful. Two men in their twenties sleep comfortably between their poor, sleep-deprived parents.*
ERIC: Should we wake them?
AMY: No way! How could you think such terrible thoughts?
ERIC: It's just that . . . I don't know . . . I was just—
AMY: Shut up! They're stirring.

Just then Wyatt, a young man of twenty-five, bolts upright in bed and screams.

WYATT: Can't you people see I'm trying to sleep?
ERIC: Sorry, son, your beard has rubbed my poor old back raw!
AMY: Oh, Eric, how could you say such a hurtful thing?
ERIC: Amy, I am just trying to get some rest.

Just then another well-rested man of twenty bolts up in bed and screams.

DUSTY: Will all of you shut up!!!

Eric and Amy cower under the covers of their 8" share of mattress. From under the covers we hear a whimper:

ERIC: We just thought maybe you guys could go sleep in your own beds for a night, that's all.

Extreme close-up on Wyatt and Dusty, who are laughing maniacally.

WYATT: Whatever, Dad.
DUSTY: Yeah, right!
AMY: Go back to sleep, honey.
ERIC: O.K. . . . . *sigh.*

ERIC'S FIVE BEST IDEAS FOR ROMANCE

My middle name is Romance. Actually it's Antony, but in Austria that means "man with ideas on how to make your master bedroom a place to rekindle that spark of passion that first attracted you to that person sleeping next to you that you can finally see because your kids are now sleeping in their own beds," but said with a thick, Schwarzeneggerian accent.

I say it's time to take back the bedroom! Get 'em out and get their stuff out, too. Reclaim your space and honor your relationship again. There are several tips that work wonders for the relationship. I know— I did it and shortly thereafter my wife gave birth to our second son. But I still know, O.K.? Back off! Here are my five best recipes for Master Bedroom Romance.

1. **Picture your romance**. Only hang pictures from your romance as a couple; make it your room, not theirs. Again, this is your space for your time together. Your kids will feel much better about themselves if they see you hugging your spouse because you want to, not because you should. Kids would much rather see you get along than see a bunch of pictures of themselves in your room.

2. **Channel your own reality**. Make the TV disappear, either behind closed doors or in another room. I make my living on TV, but that doesn't mean the TV should become a replacement for intimacy. Nor should it become a design feature. The TV (even the look of it) is distracting and numbing to the senses. It can sometimes make you check out and become unavailable. If you must have the TV in the bedroom, make sure that you guys are both in agreement that you don't want to talk or relate to each other. Sometimes there is nothing better than cozying up with your spouse and kids and watching a great movie. Or one of my TV shows. And if you do not care to hide or move the TV, consider one of many DVDs that can turn your TV into an art or photo display. When not in use as a TV, the screen will show a beautiful painting by Monet or some great photo of you guys as a couple.

3. **Struck by lighting**. Replace light switches with dimmers. Mood lighting is key. It can make all the difference in how we perceive each other. Alternative lighting sources such as candles and lanterns are also great choices. Creating a peaceful and romantic mood invites communication and intimacy. What better way to spend a quiet spa-like evening with someone you created so much life with? As my mentor for romance, the incomparable soul singer Teddy Pendergrass said, "Turn out the lights, light a candle." Boom! Two kids later, here I am! It works, thanks to lighting.

4. **Cozy blankets**. Build or buy a trunk for the foot of the bed and use it for cozy throw blanket storage—she's always cold, he's always warm. The combo = hot! Yikes! There is nothing better than a little late-afternoon nap under a cozy blanket for two. What happens before or after is your business. But I'm just going to warn you, stuff happens under cozy blankets and I just can't be held responsible. Please fill out the following waiver and send it back to me ASAP.

Eric Stromer
1531 I'm-in-Love-Again Lane
Passion Place, Virginia 69695

PASSION WAIVER
I, [your name], do solemnly swear to not hold Eric Stromer responsible for the heat and passion that may occur due to his trunk at the foot of the bed and all its contents.
Signed,
[Your name here]

5. **Fresh flowers**. Always keep fresh flowers in your bedroom. Flowers require you to pay attention to beauty—get it? We all respond to beauty; we always have and we always will. Any object that hooks you into noticing what is beautiful and what moves you is worth its weight in relationship gold.

4.
The
Rumpus
Room

RUMPUS . . . IS THAT a technical term? Take two *rumpuses* and call me in the morning? Exactly what part of the home is the *rumpus?*

I like to think of the rumpus room as more a state of mind than a physical space with four walls, a floor, and a ceiling. If you're a parent, you know kids love to sing . . . dance . . . run . . . jump . . . scream . . . cry . . . rat each other out and, well, you know, create a *ruckus.*

The ancient secret for successfully handling that ruckus (without losing your mind) . . . is the rumpus room. That's right, I said it: *rumpus room.* This is where all the magic happens. Where ideas are conceived, songs are written, plays are performed, and dances are choreographed. Picture the family hub, the place where everyone hangs out and does their thing. The work, play, kick-back, relax, party-central nerve center of all your lives.

What? You think you don't have a nerve center?

Trust me. If you have kids, they're giving your nerve center a thorough, daily workout. Want to make a little sense out of that? No sweat . . . that's why I'm here.

The rumpus room can be located in your basement, attic, family room, extra bedroom, or even a corner of living space dedicated to something else. It can also be a movable space set up for an afternoon or weekend of fun, then taken down and stowed away. Remember, we're talking *state of mind* here, not matter. What *does* matter is that this space be kid-friendly.

The basic rules for kid-friendly are bright colors, soft, plush furniture, stain-resistant fabrics, and no sharp corners. Translation: no metal-studded antique Italian lounge covered in lemon silk.

What else makes a great rumpus room? Any room that includes as many of the following items as possible:

- Pillows for "legal" pillow fights . . . and extra seating
- Removable and usable wall decor (gameboards, etc.)
- Organized displays (trophy cases, ideas for collectors, etc.)
- Lofts (think inside tree house—kids love to climb)
- Long and short fabric with clips and beams for making tents and forts
- A kids' "do job" garage or toy chest—the place you keep project materials before your brood is ready to tackle them
- A riser with wings and a curtain and lights for putting on plays
- A play oven for the younger kids

Here are my favorite versions of some of these rumpus room elements.

"ALL THE WORLD'S A STAGE" ACTIVITY CENTER

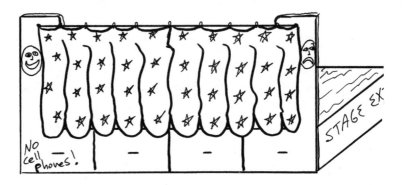

All the world's a stage, right? To a kid it is!

And you and your kids can have the best darn stage anywhere . . . anytime, with just a little work from Mom and Dad and the rest of your crew. Two separate 4'-square risers are the foundation of my design because they are portable and easy to build. Put them together to create one 4' x 8' stage or keep them separate for two 4' x 4' stages.

MATERIALS LIST

 3 sheets of plywood, 3/4" thick

 1 box of 1½" deck screws

 Carpenter's glue

 8 sturdy handles for easy transport

 1 roll of clothesline rope

 Two 3' x 8' pieces of fabric of your choice for the curtain

 1 package of clip-on curtain rings

 2 eyehooks

 1 gallon of primer

 Assorted semi-gloss latex or acrylic artist paint (colors of your choice)

Adding Costumes

My kids love to perform to music and dance and scream and carry on as long as I let them. Costumes hung on pegs can keep any area organized and add to the look of the stage. Friends can come over and select their own costumes to tell their own stories. The process of gathering the adults to watch the show is sweet, and who knows—maybe you'll create a future American idol? Nothing can kill two hours better than kids creating a show while the parents hide in the kitchen and count their blessings for actually constructing this stage in the first place.

TOOLS

- Power drill/screwdriver
- Skill saw (optional)
- Jigsaw (optional)
- Tape measure
- Pencil and straightedge or chalk line
- Paint roller
- Paintbrush
- One dose of creativity and artistic genius
- Safety glasses

A stage play area can be simple and basic (remember, imagination is half the fun) or can be expanded to have it all: a stage with wings, a real working curtain, spotlights, oversize-seating devices, and a full costume area.

Plan to construct a stage based on the size of the area you have available. Don't worry if you have to size down your stage due to limited play space. The magic comes from within your little merrymakers, not the materials. And, rest assured, no matter what size stage you construct, there is always some magic left over for Mom and Dad, as this stage project can buy adults oodles of time together.

The secret? Two simple words: "Keep rehearsing."

You'll find that the rehearsal process can keep your little thespians busy just long enough to get you through an entire adult dinner party!

INSTRUCTIONS

1. Ask your lumberyard to cut one of the sheets of birch plywood into four 1' x 8' lengths, or use the skill saw to do it yourself.

2. You now have four 1' x 8' plywood strips and two full sheets of birch plywood left over. For now, set the full sheets aside and concentrate on the strips.

3. Crosscut each of the four strips in half, making eight pieces 1' x 4'. Set aside four of those pieces. Trim off 1¹/₂" from the short edge of the remaining four strips to make them each a size of 1' x 3'10¹/₂".

4. The finished outside dimensions of each box will be 4' x 4'. To achieve the correct size, each box combines two shorter pieces with two longer pieces.

5. Cut one more 1' x 8' strip off of your second whole sheet of plywood. You'll be left with a 3' x 8' sheet and the off-cut piece. This off-cut piece will be used as a center support in each of your boxes. Cut the 1' x 8' piece into two 1' x 4' pieces. Then trim the short edge of each piece to 3'10¹/₂".

You are now ready to assemble the frame of your two risers. Here's how they should lay out.

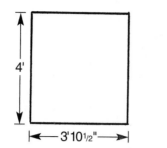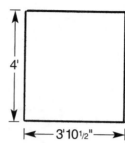

6. To begin, take one 4' length and one 3'10½" length. Apply a thin layer of carpenter's glue to one end of the 3'10½" length. Line that end up against one end of the 4' length to create a right angle.

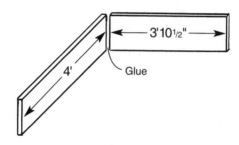

7. Brace the short end against something firm on your workbench. Use the power screwdriver to drive four evenly spaced screws through the 4' length to secure the two pieces together. Continue to assemble the box shape by applying glue to the short piece and inserting four evenly spaced screws in the long piece. When you have finished the first box, simply repeat these steps to complete the second one. When you are finished, you will have two boxes 4' x 4' outside dimensions.

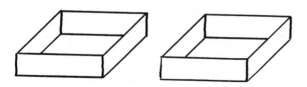

8. Next insert the center support piece and attach with glue and four evenly spaced screws.

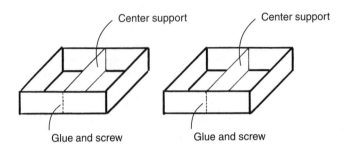

9. Finally, take your last remaining sheet of plywood and crosscut it in half. You should now have two pieces 4' x 4'. These pieces will complete the box part of the risers.

10. Spread a thin bead of glue along the top edge of your box frame, including along the center support piece. Carefully lay the top in place and fasten to the frame with screws spaced 6" apart around the perimeter and down the center into your center support.

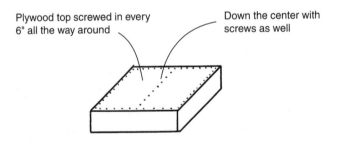

11. Congratulations! You should now have two 4' x 4' risers with tops. The next step is to construct the stage wings.

12. You will use the remaining 3' x 8' piece of plywood. Begin by cutting it into two 3' x 4' pieces. The wings should have a whimsical shape to them. I like to use a jigsaw to give the wings a smooth but creative

shape. Now, reach deep down inside and find your creative urge. Trust me, it's there or you wouldn't have made it this far. Now is the time to deploy it.

13. Cut your first wing into a shape something like this.

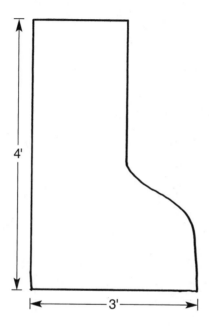

14. Now, place that on top of the other piece of plywood and trace the outline onto the full 3' x 4' piece. After cutting this second piece you will have a matching pair of wings.

15. Next, fasten one wing to each riser using the glue and screw (four evenly spaced screws) method.

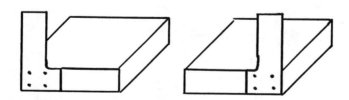

16. Screw your handles to the front and back of the riser.

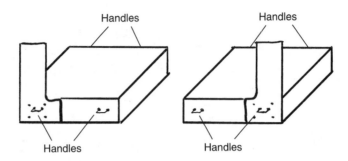

17. Attach the eyehooks on the top outside corners of your wings.

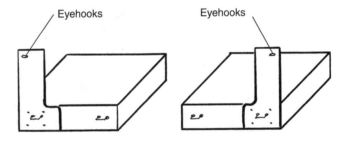

18. Prime and paint the stage and wings using as much creativity as possible. I'm talking red, blue, yellow . . . circles . . . symbols . . . moons, stars, and planets . . . names . . . animals . . . whatever your family can think of. Your imagination has no limit.

Ways to Amp It Up

Use masking tape to block off a section on the front of the wings and paint with several coats of blackboard paint. Now your little darlings can change the "Now Playing" bill each time they set out to perform!

19. Clip curtain rings to your curtains every 6".

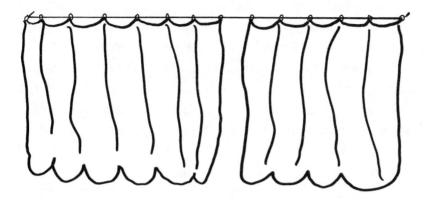

20. Thread the clothesline through the rings and tie off to the wings in the eyehooks.

THE MINI-VIKING KITCHEN CENTER

When the kids in your house span a range of ages, the young ones often don't make the cut into the older one's theatrical plans. It's heartbreaking, but there's an even bigger problem: the younger ones come back to *you* for entertainment. . . .

Every parent knows there's a magic hour—daily around 5 P.M. or any time company visits—when you are in the kitchen preparing a feast, trying to enjoy some quality time with your spouse or guests. This is the *exact* moment when the small fry descend on you, demanding juice . . . yogurt . . . string cheese . . .

Face it: *you'd give them your ATM card if they asked.* The problem is that while you're trying to meet their demands, the tipsy just-learning-to-walk toddler tilts in your direction and becomes entangled between your legs.

As you fall toward the refrigerator there is that "Aha!" moment, a vision of an organized play area within sight, in the kitchen, but far enough away so you can prepare dinner, socialize, or have five minutes of kid-free time. I call this the Mini-Viking Kitchen Center!

The dinner hour is extremely challenging for moms and dads. The Mini-Viking Kitchen Center is the *only* distraction that I have found to work in the Stromer home during dinner preparation. All you need are a few dollars in lumber and you're on your way to a hassle-free dinner! Since introducing the toy oven into our kitchen two years ago, my wife and I have had at least fifteen minutes of conversation. When was the last time you had a conversation with your spouse that didn't contain the phrases "put that down" or "stop pushing in your brother's soft spot"? I'm here to tell you that a kitchen corner dedicated to your child is a stroke of genius that you will not regret.

Getting the Younger Ones Cooking

The Mini-Viking Kitchen Center is easy and fun to build. Add plastic fruit, vegetables, meats, and cheeses and you've created a place for the toddlers to hang out and practice their culinary skills alongside Mom and Dad.

Watch in complete awe as your child prepares little plastic meals using toy fruit, pork chops, and fake lettuce and bread. After your culinary genius prepares his faux meal, he will thrill you with his aim as he lobs plastic bacon at your six-year-old, who, for once, is quietly drawing a picture at the kitchen table!

This miracle play center can also double as a percussion area. Slip in your earplugs and let your youngest clank little pots and pans together. You can bet the frenetic groove will escalate into total madness just before dinner is served. *Bon appétit.*

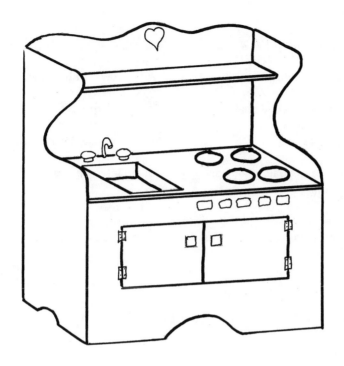

MATERIALS LIST

 Two 1" x 12" x 10' pine boards

 One 4' x 4' sheet of ⅛" luan

 4 cabinet door hinges

 1 box of 1½" finishing nails and 1 box of 1½" drywall screws

80–120 grit sandpaper, variety pack

 Carpenter's glue

 50 pine screw hole plugs

 One 8" x 8" plastic storage container for the sink

 Assorted plastic or wood toy food, pots, pans, etc.

TOOLS

Router* (optional)

Jigsaw and wood blade set*

Tape measure

Pencil and straightedge or chalk line

Power drill/screwdriver

¹/₈" drill bit

¹/₂" countersink drill bit

Safety glasses

*GEAR ALERT: These tools are a must-have for advanced woodworking. They're also really fun to use!

INSTRUCTIONS

Mini-Viking Cut List

Lay out your two pine boards and begin measuring and cutting out all the pieces listed below. As you cut, carefully label each piece as indicated. This will help you during the assembly phase of construction.

A. 2 pieces 3' x 11¹/₂", labeled A-1 and A-2.

B. A piece 2' x 6¹/₂" (from off-cut of step 1), labeled B.

C. From the same piece off-cut another piece 2' x 3¹/₂", labeled G.

D. 2 pieces 2' x 5¹/₂", labeled C and E.

E. A piece 2' x 11¹/₂", labeled D.

F. A piece 2' x 11¹/₂", labeled F.

G. A piece 2' x 9¹/₂" labeled K. (Use off-cut from this step for next step.)

H. 2 pieces 9" x 11¹/₂", labeled H-1 and H-2.

I. 2 pieces 11" x 11", labeled I-1 and I-2.

J. A piece 9¹/₂" x 2', labeled J. (Use off-cut for knobs.)

K. A piece of luan 16" x 2', labeled L. (Use off-cut for burners.)

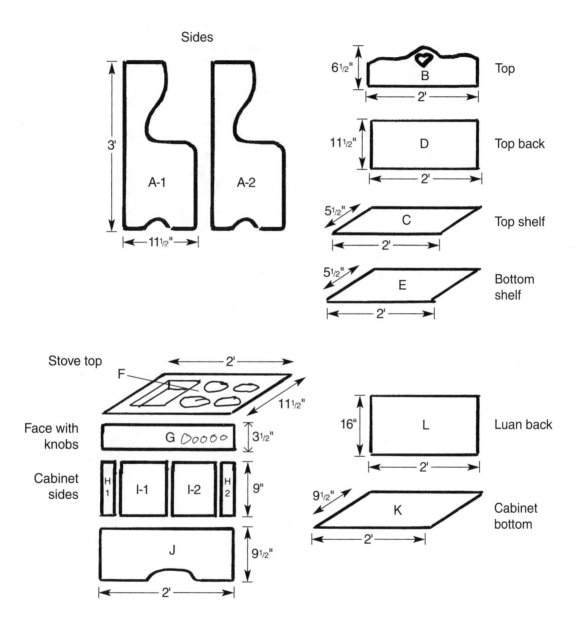

Sides

3'

A-1   A-2

11½"

6½"   B   Top

2'

11½"   D   Top back

2'

5½"   C   Top shelf

2'

5½"   E   Bottom shelf

2'

Stove top

F

2'

11½"

Face with knobs   G   3½"

Cabinet sides   H1   I-1   I-2   H2   9"

J   9½"

2'

16"   L   Luan back

2'

9½"   K   Cabinet bottom

2'

Knob and Faucet Cuts

2. From your off-cuts and leftovers, cut out oven knobs.
For front of stove, cut four knobs 1½" x 1½".
For the oven controller and hot and cold water, cut three 2" x 2".

3. Cut out a faucet from off-cuts that is L-shaped. Use the sandpaper to sand off the rough edges, then glue in place on piece F.

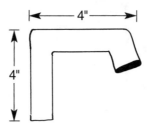

4. Pre-drill a hole through the center of each of the knobs, and then attach to the oven with a screw through the middle. Don't tighten completely so that the knobs can turn on the screw.

Gussy up your oven by making the following cuts.

5. On pieces A-1 and A-2 draw these curves. Draw the curves freehand on the first piece, then flip it over and trace the exact curves on the second piece.

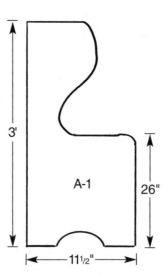

Cut to Your Heart's Content

To cut out the heart shape, draw it in place first. Then pre-drill inside the line with a ⅛" drill bit. You want to create a hole big enough for the blade of your jigsaw blade to fit inside. Insert the jigsaw and carefully cut out the heart shape. Don't worry if it's not perfect. Not only will sandpaper do wonders, but slight imperfections will only add to the charm.

6. On piece B, draw these curves.

Note: This is easier than it looks. Your only requirement is that the sides be 4¹/₂" tall and the middle be 6¹/₂" tall.

7. Now it's time to work on the stove-top piece labeled F. Lay out your plastic food container on the left side.

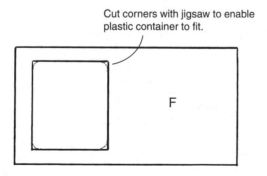

Cut corners with jigsaw to enable plastic container to fit.

F

Trace around the bottom of the container in the desired location. Pre-drill on the line with a ¹/8" drill bit. Then insert the jigsaw blade and begin to cut out the insert hole. Cut until the container sits flat in the hole. The opening will roughly be 8" x 8".

8. On your piece labeled J, trace out a scallop.

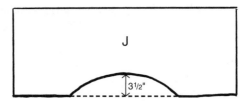

Mini-Viking Pre-drill Holes

9. You know those toys you buy that say "some assembly required"? And when you open the box, what you find are stacks of wood pieces with pre-drilled holes and plastic bags of screws, bolts, nuts, etc.? Basically, what you are doing in this step is making all the pre-drilled holes.

These are the approximate pre-drill points where all of the shelves and pieces will connect. Use a countersink drill bit, approximately ¹/2" in diameter.

Mini-Viking Assembly Instructions

10. Take A-1 and lay it on your work surface.

11. Pre-assemble (pre-drill and glue) piece B and piece C together to create a right angle, with B sitting on top of C at an edge.

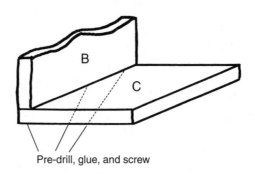

Pre-drill, glue, and screw

12. Attach A-1 to the B and C combo.

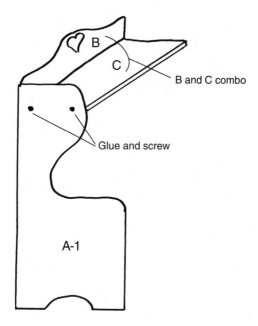

13. Take piece labeled D and attach it directly below the B and C combo.

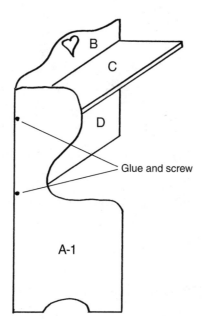

14. Attach piece labeled F.

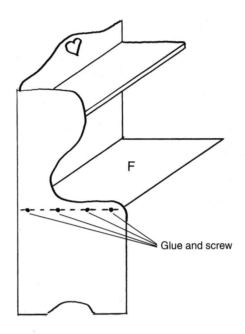

Glue and screw

15. Go ahead and attach the other side (A-2) now.

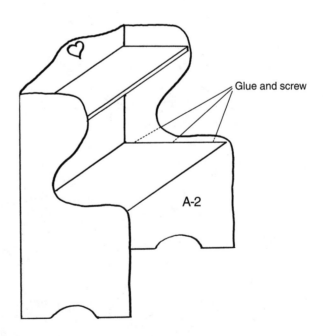

Glue and screw

A-2

16. To install the lower shelf, piece E: On the outside of pieces A-1 and A-2 measure 14 1/2" from the floor up. Mark across with a pencil. Pre-drill two holes, 4" apart on both pieces A-1 and A-2. Slide shelf E into place and secure by screwing into holes on each side.

To install the bottom, piece K: On the outside of pieces A-1 and A-2 measure 7" from the floor up. Mark across with a pencil. Pre-drill three holes, 4" apart on both pieces A-1 and A-2. Insert bottom shelf K and secure with screws into the holes on each side.

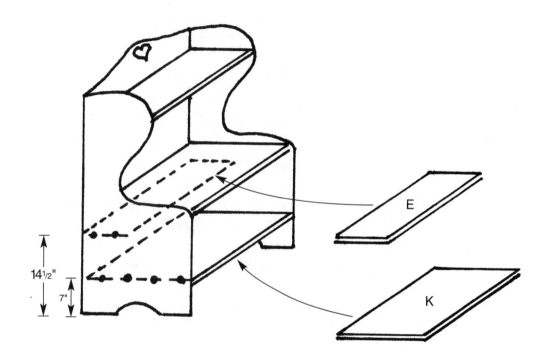

17. Attach pieces G, H-1, J, and H-2 as shown.

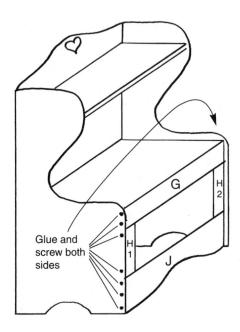

18. Turn the oven front away from you and attach the luan sheathing (labeled L) at the broken lines indicated in the illustration. You are going to glue and nail the backing into place along the back edges of the bottom shelf (K), middle shelf (E), and top back (D).

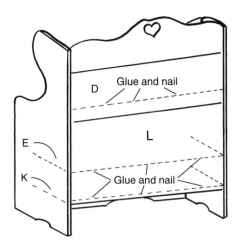

19. First run a thin bead of the carpenter's glue along the edge of the shelf. Then position the luan in place. Next, you will secure the backing with the 1½" finishing nails spaced 4" apart.

20. Turn the oven around to face you and you're ready to install the oven doors. Attach door pieces (I-1 and I-2) to the front of H-1 and H-2 with the hinges. Note: the doors are cut to be larger than the hole so that they don't fit inside, but overlay on the outside. Set aside the knobs for your oven: four pieces 1½" x 1½" and three pieces 2" x 2".

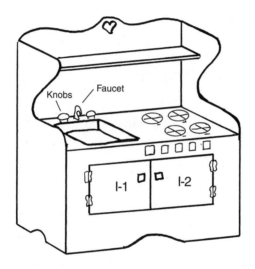

21. To create the burners, cut the leftover luan into four 4" x 4" squares. If you're feeling *daring*, round these out by sanding off the corners. Glue the burners in place on your stove top.

22. Insert the plastic container sink and plastic food and the fake cooking can begin.

Soon, you'll be the envy of all your neighbors as they line up to taste your child's delicious plastic lasagna, with a side of plastic bacon and a plastic chicken leg. Wow!

Mini-Viking Kitchen Center Shortcut: Under Threes I know you really wanted to tackle the kitchen center. You probably will, *someday*, when life cuts you a little slack. In the meantime, how about a shortcut to get you through that important dinner party . . . TONIGHT!

Start by raiding your kitchen. Check the plastic container drawer, where you probably have a large square or rectangle-shape food saver that can be pressed into action for the sink. This will not only save on the expense, but is one less thing for your shopping list. Pull out some of your smaller pots and nonbreakable cookware, too. Trust me, these will come in handy.

For our shortcut, we're going to get creative and streamline the job by employing a large packing box. It might sound like a cliché, but with kids it's true: the box is half the fun and their imagination supplies the rest. TV, appliance, or furniture packing boxes tend to be quite strong and some are even reinforced with small strips of wood. A rectangular box will work best for this design.

MATERIALS LIST

- 1 large TV or furniture packing box (You should be able to get one or the other free at your friendly home appliance or furniture store.)
- Aluminum foil (large box)
- Bottle of white craft glue
- Plastic toy food (optional)
- Sturdy non-squishable fruit, such as apples, citrus, etc. (optional)
- Paper plates
- 2" paintbrush
- Small amount of flat black paint

Box cutter

Duct tape

Tape measure

Indelible marker

Pencil and straightedge or
chalk line

Safety glasses

INSTRUCTIONS

1. Begin by shaping the box and cutting it down to the proper size. The sturdy bottom of the box will become the TOP of your stove. Cut off top flaps. Measure the height of the box against your toddler and cut down the sides until you have a reasonable play area height.

2. Measure the distance from the bottom of the left side, over the top, and down to the bottom of the right side. Then add 6" to this number. This is the length of aluminum foil you will need to cover both sides and the top. Measure and cut the foil to this size. You might need to cut two (or more) lengths of foil, depending on the width of your box and the width of your foil. Set aside these cut pieces of foil.

3. Next, measure from the bottom front of your box up, across the top, and down the back to the floor. Add 6" to this figure, too. Measure and cut the foil. Cut enough strips to cover the width of your box and to allow for 2" to lap over on each side.

4. Pour about 1/2 cup of the white glue into a paper cup and add 1/4 cup of water to make it thin and easy to spread. Stir well with a stick. Brush a thin layer of this glue mixture on both left and right sides of the box and across the top.

5. Working quickly before the glue dries, position the aluminum

foil on the top and down each side. Press into place with your hands. Turn the extra up under the edge of the box and crimp in place. Smooth with your hands or use a rolling pin.

6. Repeat the glue application and aluminum foil to the front, top, and back of your stove. Give most of your attention to smoothing the foil on the top of the box, this is the area that will get the most workouts. (Clean the glue out of your paintbrush with warm, soapy water, as you will need it later for painting.)

7. Once the foil has had about 30 minutes to dry in place, you can begin to add character to your box. Lightly trace around your plastic food keeper in place for the sink, but don't cut out the shape. Instead find a point in the center of the sink space and draw an X that extends across the center from each corner. Use the box cutter to cut on this X. Do NOT remove the pieces. Instead, carefully press and fold the triangle shapes into the hole as you gently press and fit the plastic container into place.

8. Once the plastic food container is neatly in the hole, turn the unit upside down. Cut five or six strips of the duct tape and use them to tape the cardboard triangles of the box to the plastic food container. This should hold the plastic sink in place, and keeping the cardboard triangles in place will add some strength to the sink and (hopefully) keep it from pushing through. Just remember, this is a temporary setup and only made of cardboard. At some point, it's gonna go.

9. Use the paintbrush to paint two paper plates with the flat black paint. Let dry for 30 minutes, then glue plates to the top of the box to simulate burners. Add the fake food or sturdy fruit and *voilà*!

Now you're cooking . . . and so are your small fry.

THE KIDSTER'S LAST STAND MOVABLE FORT

During the last six years of my life I have spent at least four of them in a child's tent or fort. Kids love to build, design, and create. Whenever my son has a playdate, I end up doing his and his friend's grunt work and designing, building, and sitting under some elaborate fabric and pillow combination.

The fun to be had with this Movable Fort is only limited by your space and the amount of fabric or sheets you're willing to make available for play. Once I discovered where all of our sheets and towels had disappeared to, I was inspired to create the "tools" for the world's greatest (and fastest) fort.

The only building required for this project is the construction of two simple wooden base units.

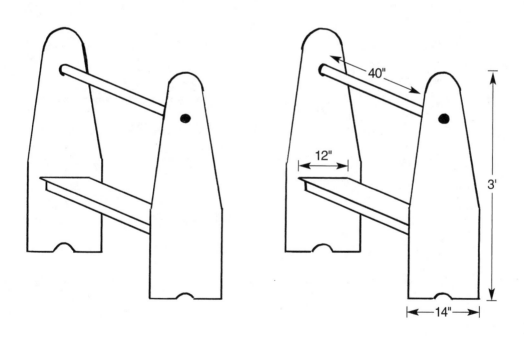

MATERIALS LIST

 1 sheet of plywood, 3/4" thick

 One 3/4" wood dowel, 8' long

 1 box of 1½" drywall screws or 1½" finishing nails

 Carpenter's glue

 3/4" drill bit

 Assorted fabric or sheets for draping

 4 or more spring-loaded tension clamps to hold fabric in place* (optional)

*These clamps resemble clothespins on steroids and are available in the clamps department of your local hardware store.

TOOLS

 Circular saw or table saw

 Jigsaw

 Hammer or nail gun and compressor

 Tape measure

 Pencil and straightedge or chalk line

 Power drill/screwdriver

 Safety glasses

Fort Base Unit Assembly Instructions

1. Out of the sheet of plywood, cut four pieces 3' long by 14" wide. The top edge is curved.

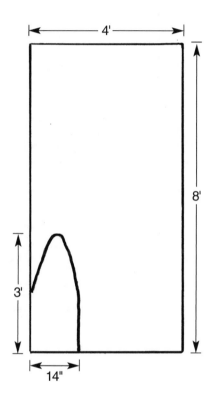

Making Things Match

A great trick for making the curves match: draw and cut out one, then use it as a guide to trace the other three.

2. You can get three of the four pieces you need by lining them up along the narrow 4' side of your plywood. This will leave a 5' x 4' piece of plywood. Cut the fourth piece from this remainder.

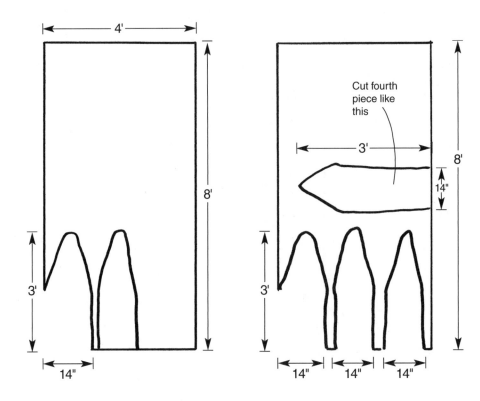

3. Next, cut two shelves 3'4" x 12".

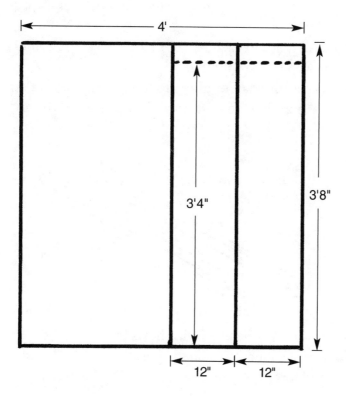

4. Take your off-cut and cut four pieces 1" x 3'4".

Instructions for Assembly of Base Unit Bottom Shelf

5. Use a tape measure to mark eight spots on each 1" x 3'4" strip, 6" apart.

6. Pre-drill holes in each one of these marks. Pre-drilling helps to prevent the wood from splitting.

7. Apply a thin bead of glue along one edge of the strip. Then apply it to the underside of the shelf. Recess the strip 3/4" from the side.

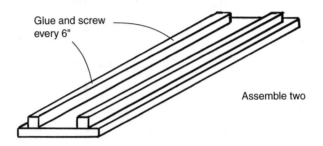

Glue and screw every 6"

Assemble two

8. Screw through the pre-drilled holes to firmly attach the shelf.

9. Lay one of your cutouts on its side and attach 12" up from the bottom. Pre-drill three holes in the side piece. And don't forget to glue before you screw.

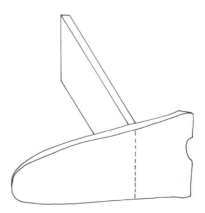

10. Cut two dowel pieces to 41½" lengths.

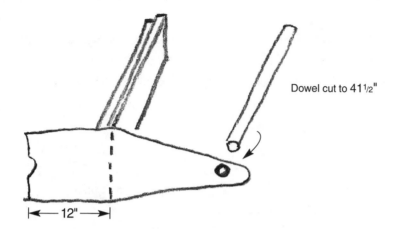

Dowel cut to 41½"

12"

11. Drill a ¾" hole from the top end of your base unit. Line the inside with glue and insert the dowel. Twist into place. Refer to the illustration for steps 5 to 7. The dowel should fit flush with the outside edge of the side piece.

Note: You may have to bore out your hole slightly larger than ¾" so that the dowel will fit in easily.

12. Glue and screw the other side piece in place.

13. Congrats! Now build the other one.

14. Attach your fabric or sheet and crawl into your fort and enjoy!

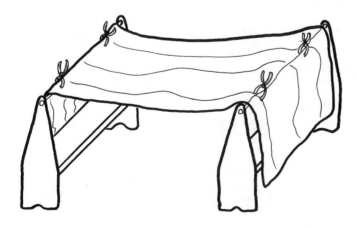

Movable Fort Shortcut: Under Threes While the base units for my Movable Fort instructions are simple, sometimes you just have enough resources to gut it out, quick and dirty. And you know what? That's O.K. The little ones will love your abbreviated effort just as well.

For my Movable Fort shortcut I rely on plastic sawhorses, which run about $30 a pair, and a couple of tension clamps.

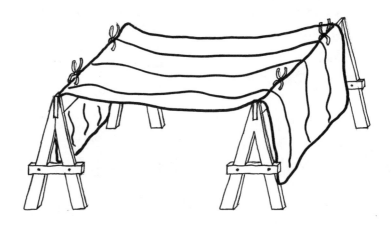

MATERIALS LIST

 A pair of plastic sawhorses

 4 or more spring-loaded tension clamps to hold fabric in place* (optional)

 Pillows (optional—what the heck, get them from the bed, too)

 Assorted sheets (take them off the bed if you have to, it will give you something to laugh about later)

*These clamps resemble clothespins on steroids and are available in the clamps department of your local hardware store.

Your bare hands are more than enough.

1. Line up the plastic sawhorses in close proximity.
2. Drape with fabric and clamp in place.
3. Load with kids . . . wait for giggling to occur. Get camera and document this unbridled family moment.

EXPANDABLE GROWTH CHART

I was first introduced to the idea of a growth chart when I was around four. My family would spend time every summer in a beautiful town called Lac du Flambeau, Wisconsin, on Crawling Stone Lake. The 1940s cottage where we stayed had thirty or forty years of pencil marks on the back of the basement door.

This record of generations of other boys and girls on the back of the old pine door was something I looked forward to seeing every summer. Before long, my brother and I started charting our progress there as well.

By the time we all moved to the West Coast to start our adult lives, I thought about that growth chart and wished I could have saved it to compare with my sons' growth, giving them a chance to keep a little part of my past for themselves. Plus, I liked the idea of recording height, but wanted to add other details to reflect my kids' development.

The Expandable Growth Chart found here allows you and your children to track their height, but also their *size*. I like to trace the outline of my kids' hands and then fill in the lines with paint. This is a great way to compare height with size.

The design is simple and really fun to build. A series of wood pegs and holes drilled every inch gives your children the ability to stand under a pre-drilled hole and gives you an easy tape-measure-free way to chart their height. And because 1/4", 1/2", 3/4", and 1" increments are clearly marked on our growth chart, all you have to do is plug a 1/4" wood dowel into the pre-drilled hole, position your child under it, then mark the spot on the growth chart.

It's also fun to decorate the chart with pictures of healthy food groups to encourage your kids to make healthy food choices. You can also add the height of some of your favorite movie or sport stars. By the way, I'm 6'2". Make sure that goes on there!

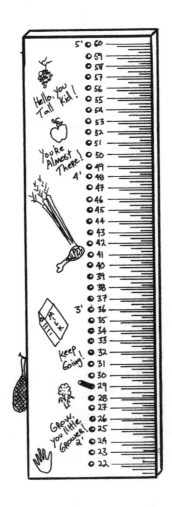

- One 1" x 12" x 8' piece of clear pine (no knots)
- One 12" length of 1/4"-diameter wood dowel
- 2 drywall anchors and screws or two 1½" drywall screws
- 1 small pouch to hold pegs

TOOLS

- Circular saw or chop saw
- Power drill/screwdriver with Phillips head tip
- 1/4" drill bit
- Tape measure
- Pencil and straightedge
- Paint or clear coat
- Indelible black marker
- Safety glasses

INSTRUCTIONS

1. Cut 1" x 12" x 8' pine board to fit in desired location. That could be on a wall above the floor molding and below the ceiling or, if your kid is already at least 24" tall, you may just want to hang the growth chart 24" from the floor and whatever is left to the ceiling is your finished measurement (just be sure to begin your measurements at 24" and then hang your chart up the wall). This means that if you have a standard eight-foot ceiling, you will cut the pine board down to 5' or 6'.

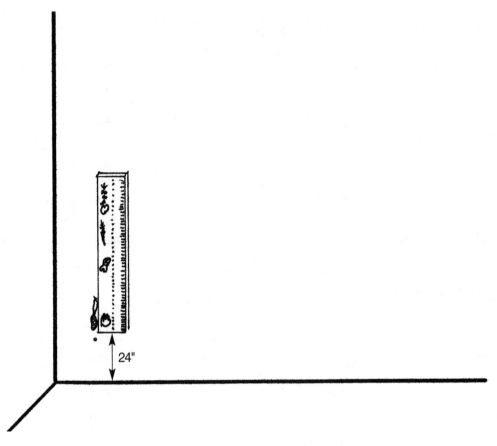

24"

2. Before installation, pre-drill your growth chart 2" from the top and 2" from the bottom. Hold the growth chart to the wall and, with a level, make sure it is plumb (hanging straight up and down). Mark a light line with a pencil down one side of the chart so you can remove it and then replace it on the wall without having to use the level again.

3. Drop the level to the floor and put your growth chart against the wall again. Use your pencil tip to mark those pre-drilled holes at the top and bottom of your growth chart.

4. Put the growth chart aside and place your drywall anchor on the Phillips head tip of your screw gun. Drill into the drywall with the anchor until it sits just on the surface of the drywall, exactly where you marked the wall for the top and bottom of the chart.

5. Now you can place your growth chart back on the wall; line it up with the pencil marks and with your holes. Insert the screw part of the drywall anchor combination through the hole of the growth chart and into the drywall anchor embedded in the wall. Screw very loosely to temporarily hold it in place so you can walk away and it will stay on the wall all by itself.

6. Use your tape measure and calculate your marks from the floor up to where your growth chart starts. Make marks with a pencil at every foot, inch, 3/4", 1/2", and 1/4".

7. Unscrew the top screw and take your growth chart to an area where you will work on it and make a bit of a mess, such as your personal workshop area.

8. Lay it down on a work surface and highlight every 1" increment with a pencil mark.

9. Draw a line down the center of the growth chart from top to bottom. Also, draw a line from top to bottom on the edge of your growth chart 1" from the edge. Transfer all your 1" increment marks to that center line and the edge line.

10. Grab a 1/4" drill bit from your toolbox. Measure up from the tip of your drill bit 1/2" toward the drill. Take a piece of tape about an inch and a half long and wrap it around the drill bit. This is like putting an adhesive bandage around your finger at that 1/2" point—it gives you a depth gauge so you'll know how deep to drill down into your growth chart at every 1" mark. You only want to go to the edge of your tape.

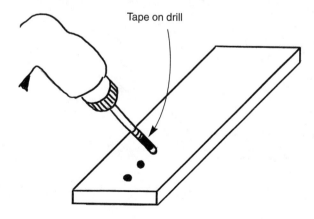
Tape on drill

11. Drill down to your tape line everywhere you marked 1". These holes ultimately will be the 1" peg indicators that you and your family will use as your little one flies up the growth chart. The center holes are to mark height and the side holes are to glue a permanent peg for lasting evidence of his or her height at that moment in time.

12. Take your section of wood dowel and cut it into 1" lengths for the permanent pegs you will glue into the side holes and a couple of 3" pegs to represent the number of kids in the family. Each kid should have his own color.

13. Paint or stain your base color. If you paint, I recommend priming first and then painting. Everybody in your Dream Team should paint his own color on all his pegs. These will hang from a pouch at the bottom of your growth chart.

14. If you're going to add the traced hand detail, do it now, and fill in with color. Let dry.

15. Now, starting from the bottom, find your first hole and draw a pencil line across both holes, right through the center going up the growth chart, like 1" ladder rungs.

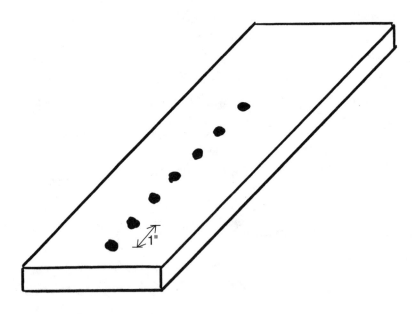

16. Draw with your colored permanent marker any words of encouragement, like "Keep going, you little grower!" Or "Hey, what are you, some kind of crazy growing machine?" You can also draw chicken legs or eggs or broccoli or anything that seems like *growing food.* Once the permanent marker has dried, you can fill it in with paint or other color permanent markers.

17. After you have completed the painting, screw your new growth chart into place.

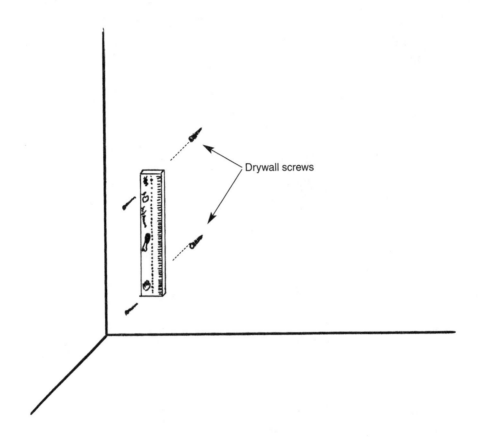

Drywall screws

Now sit back and let the growing begin!

Expandable Growth Chart Shortcut: Under Threes A faster growth chart option simply requires buying a strip of 1" x 1/4" flat wood molding. Cut your molding to fit along the inside of a doorway. Mark off the inches with a ruler and an indelible marker. Nail or screw into the door jamb. If you are going to attach it to your doorway with screws, I suggest that you pre-drill attachment holes so the molding doesn't crack. Buy stickers to decorate. Enjoy!

THE INCREDIBLE ALL-IN-ONE, SCRAPBOOKING, PRESENT-WRAPPING, COMPUTER-USING, ART-MAKING, HOME WORKSTATION

It contains clutter, stores art supplies, wrapping paper, craft supplies, a computer, and hey, it looks nice. Oh my God! What doesn't it do? It might even bring about world peace. O.K., kidding. But it can serve up *home* peace. This little project provides a simple, well-thought-out space to create and store all those family craft and art projects. This area is the creative (but chaos free) space every parent dreams of.

I find that the majority of my greatest-ever artistic achievements came about because I was lucky enough to have an environment that was conducive to creativity. Because my dad ran an art gallery, I was able to visit many artists' studios, and the one thing they all had in common was some system for organizing their art materials.

One really great storage area can organize the creative supplies of an entire family. The workstation provides a comfortable place where you can all be creative at the same time. Plus, don't forget that sometimes, when doing homework or working on the computer, a short artistic break can refocus creative energies. For all of these reasons, I think it makes sense to combine homework, art, and supply storage into one convenient station!

To begin, find an open wall where you can have a run of at least six feet, but hopefully even longer. I love the two-person desktops that allow multiple family members to use the space at the same time.

If you don't have a matching pair of two-drawer filing cabinets, go out and get some. They are inexpensive and two should provide enough space to file a family's art projects and homework assignments.

Included in the construction of this project are a wrapping paper dispenser; a unit that can either house a CPU tower or become a mid-desk shelf; two over-desk shelves; and an angled Peg-Board that can display spools of colorful thread, organize keys, and house other craft supplies.

- 2 sheets of plywood, 3/4" thick

- 1 half sheet 4' x 4' of 1/4" luan

- Two 2-drawer file cabinets (color of your choice)

- 3' length of 1/4" wood dowel

- 12' length of 1/2" wood dowel

- Six 8" shelving brackets

- 1 box of 3/4" screws

- 5 drywall anchors rated to hold 60 lbs each

- 1 box of 2" nail gun nails or 2" finishing nails

- Carpenter's glue

- Primer/paint, stain/clear coat, or furniture wax finish (see pages 25–28)

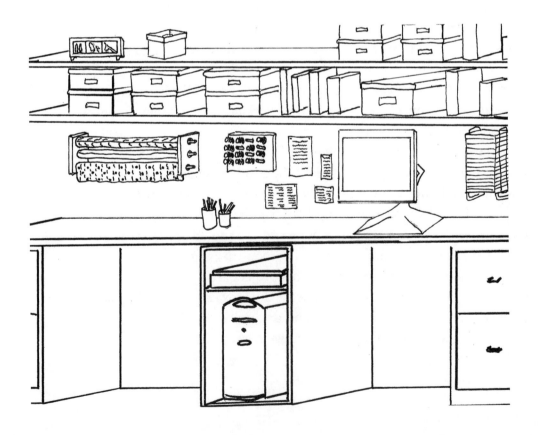

Circular saw or table saw

Screw gun with Phillips head tip

⅛", ¼", ½" drill bits

Hammer or nail gun and compressor

Tape measure

Pencil and straightedge or chalk line

45-degree-angle speed square (for step 29)

Safety glasses

INSTRUCTIONS

1. From each sheet of plywood, rip a 30" piece, a 12" piece, and a 6" piece. Stack all the like pieces together. Below is the cut list for this project.

Home Workstation template

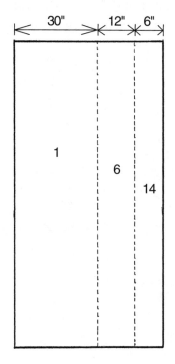

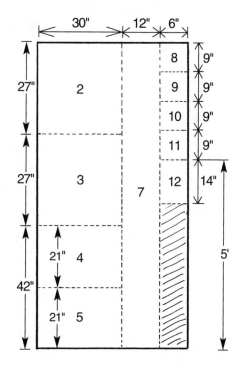

Denotes scrap

2. Take one of your 30" x 8' sheets and set it aside as your desktop. Label it 1.

3. Take a second 30" x 8' piece and crosscut to 27". Label this 2.

4. Crosscut another piece to 27" and label it 3. These two pieces will be your CPU holder sides.

5. You will be left with a piece of scrap that is 42" x 30". Take that piece and cut it in half so that both of the pieces you end up with have a dimension of 21" x 30". Label these pieces 4 and 5. They will be the top and bottom of your CPU holder.

6. Take two of your 12" x 8' pieces and set them aside for shelving. Label these 6 and 7.

7. Take one of your 6" x 8' pieces, and from it rip 9" so you have a piece that measures 9" x 6". Label this piece 8. Perform that same 9" rip 3 more times until you have a total of four 9" x 6" pieces. Label the last three pieces 9 through 11.

8. You will be left with a 5' piece that is 6" x 5'. Crosscut a piece to 14" and label it 12. This will be the base of your Peg-Board organizer.

9. Assemble the CPU box as shown using pieces 2 through 5, and the luan backing, which we will label 13. Cut the 1/4" luan backing to size and glue, then nail onto the back of the box. The luan backing keeps the box from racking or leaning to one side.

CPU Holder for Workstation

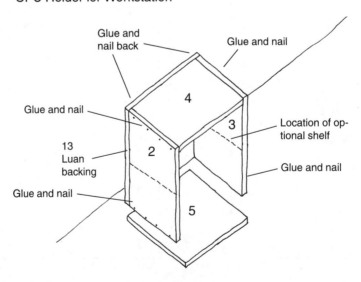

10. Now prime and paint, stain and clear coat, or wax all your cut pieces including your desktop.

11. Take your last remaining off-cut piece, 6" x 8', and label it 14. Place it horizontally on the wall where you are going to locate your artsy-craftsy center. Drop the piece on the floor and use your tape measure to calculate the height of your file cabinets and the CPU holder you just built. They should be the same. Transfer that height onto the wall and make a mark.

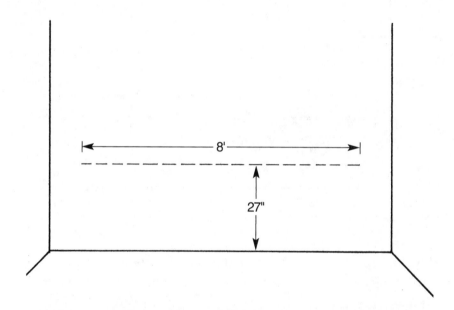

12. Now take piece 14 and hold the top edge to the wall right on the mark you made. Grab a level and rest it on the top of the 6" x 8' piece you are holding. Get the bubble in the center and trace a line along the top edge of the wood strip all the way along the 8' run.

13. While holding the piece in place, have a helper drill with a 1/8" drill bit right through the wood and into the drywall. Make five evenly spaced holes along the run of the 8'. Pull the wood away from the wall and sink your drywall anchors into the holes you just made in the drywall.

14. Put the board back up (it's called a *ledger*), line it up with the holes, and screw in your screws until the ledger is tight to the wall. Place your CPU holder right in the center of that 8' space on the floor, about 30" out from the wall.

Note: If you don't need a CPU holder, you can insert a shelf at the halfway point of this open unit and use this area for storage.

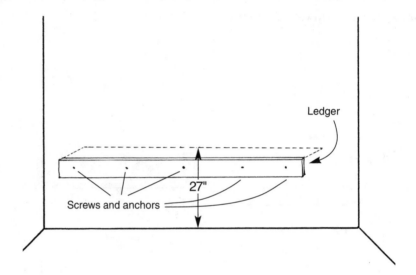

Ledger

Screws and anchors

27"

15. Arrange the file cabinets on either end of the 8' span.

16. Bring over your desktop labeled 1, lay it out on top of the cabinets, and slide it to the wall so that it's also resting on the ledger strip. Nail the back of the desktop down onto the ledger strip. Use one nail every 16".

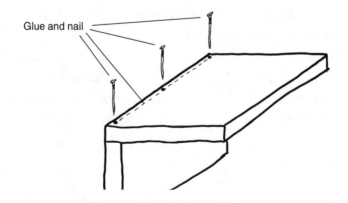

Glue and nail

17. Shoot a 1" drywall screw up through the top of the CPU holder and into the desktop. Your desk area should feel secure.

18. Next, install the shelf bracket above the desk, evenly spaced over an 8' span. Use a line that spans the whole 8' and clears your computer monitor. (Most computer monitors have a height of at least 20".) Do yourself a favor and check the height of yours before you proceed.

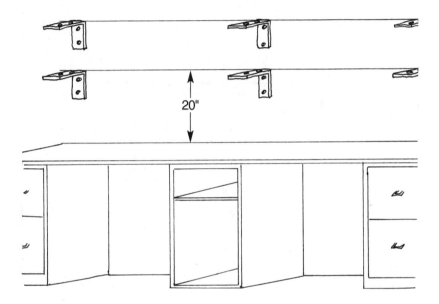

19. Put the top of your shelf brackets right on the line and make a pencil mark in the pre-drilled holes of your shelf brackets. Take the brackets away from the wall and drill in wall anchors.

20. Put your shelf bracket back and screw in the accompanying screws to secure the bracket.

Note: If the holes in the shelf brackets are too large and the head of the screw slips through, take one of your screws to the hardware store and ask them to match your screw with a tiny washer.

21. Once the two rows of brackets are in, lay your shelves across the brackets and secure the shelf to the bracket with 3/4" screws from under the shelf. Take care your screws don't poke through the top of your shelf.

22. To build the wrapping paper caddy, lay out your pre-cuts 8 through 11 on a work surface. Eight and 11 will become the dowel holders. Using a pencil and straightedge, draw a vertical line down the center of both pieces.

23. Arrange these two pieces so that the long 9" part is vertical. Measure down from the top and make a mark at these points: 2", 4^1/$_2$", and 7".

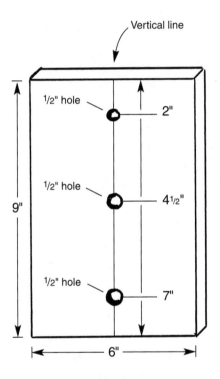

24. Drill a 1/2" hole at each of these three points on both pieces.

Stromer Slick Tip: A surefire way to safely drill all the way through a 3/4" piece of pine stock would be to layer the piece on top of another piece of scrap wood. This will allow you to comfortably plunge the drill all the way through your piece without damaging your drill bit or your work surface.

25. Numbers 9 and 10 will create the right angles, allowing you to attach the wrapping paper unit to the wall. Next, glue and nail these pieces together.

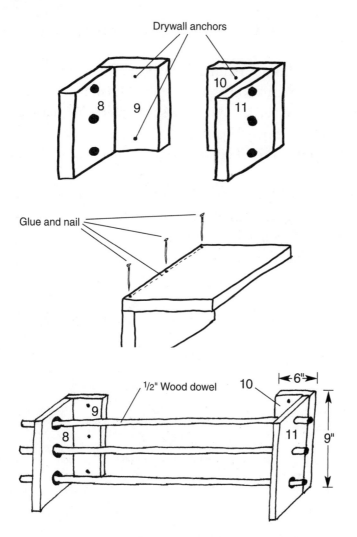

26. Fasten it to the wall with drywall anchors approximately 36" apart. It should look like a three-tier paper towel holder.

27. Cut the 1/2" diameter dowel into three pieces, each 4' long. Slide rolls of ribbon on the top dowel and rolls of wrapping paper over the

other two dowels. Slip all three dowels into place in the rack. They will stay in place because the dowels are wider than the rack. Oh my God, you can now wrap presents like the pros!

Next we will construct the angled Peg-Board organizer.

28. Lay out number 12 on a work surface. Lay it horizontally and draw four evenly spaced lines across the width of the board. Next draw five evenly spaced vertical lines across the piece. You have created an evenly spaced, 20-peg grid pattern.

29. Take your 1/4" drill bit and drill at all the points where the lines cross.

Note: You should slightly angle your holes upward so the pegs stick out at a slightly upward angle. A great way to achieve this angle would be to employ a 45-degree-angle speed square. Hold it alongside and orient your drill along that angle.

30. Find your 1/4" dowel and cut as many 11/4" lengths as you need to fill the holes.

31. Put a small bead of glue on the end of the pegs and gently tap them into the holes with a hammer.

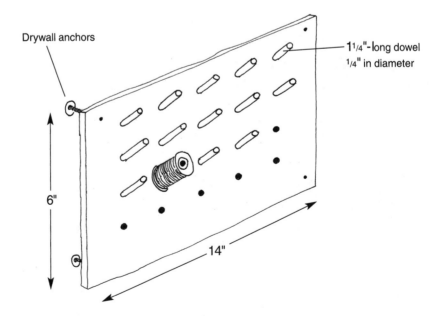

32. Pre-drill, install onto the wall, and fill with multicolored thread, various sets of keys, or other craft items.

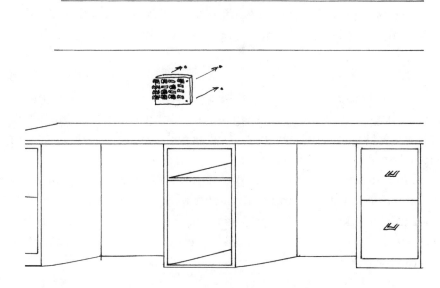

33. Now start filling up the shelves of this artsy-craftsy, coolsy-woolsy station with as many colorful clear containers as you can find. Whatever you need to make this your family's creative workstation in the *room de la rumpus*!

Art, Computer, Craft Center Shortcut: Under Threes Visit your local home-improvement store for a hollow-core door. Pick up two inexpensive filing cabinets at the office supply store. Space your filing cabinets approximately 3' apart and lay the door on top of your new cabinets. Install some prepackaged shelving above and you're on your way!

ERIC'S FIVE BEST IDEAS FOR A
FAMILY-FRIENDLY RUMPUS ROOM

The rumpus room should be conducive to the whole family. It is an all-purpose room that knows no boundaries. Here are five tips to make this indoor family playground fun, productive, and inviting.

1. **Comfort first.** Get oversize pillows that can act as seating and can also be used as crash pads for tumbling and Jerry Lewis–style pratfalls. Also, what could be better for legally thrashing a sibling than "legal" pillows? Make sure the design and fabric pattern are not too formal or expensive. Accidents will happen!

2. **Fun everywhere.** Make some of your wall-hanging decor functional gameboards by employing colorful 12" carpet squares on the floor in a checkerboard pattern as a life-size gameboard, and transform wall space into a display area for a wacky or silly hat collection. Not only will it look fun, but it will create fun as well.

3. **Fun and functional lighting.** Install lighting that can dim for your kids' theatrical productions. Then, when serious work needs to happen, you can bring the lights back up. Lighting is key in the rumpus room.

4. **Display with pride.** When your kids start to excel creatively, physically, and emotionally due to the brilliance of my rumpus room ideas, your family will require a place where all of their awards, trophies, and accomplishments can be featured. I love large corkboards for this purpose. Even a sheet of cork placed on the wall with simple adhesive provides your family with an instant place to pin up the latest article about the genius-level accomplishments of your five-year-old. After all, kids love to see their accomplishments celebrated. And guess what? We do, too.

5. **Feel free to laugh.** The other reason I love cork is because it can dampen some of the rumpusing noise created in the rumpus room. For extra soundproofing, consider lining your room with heavy drapes from floor to ceiling, 3 to 4" from the wall. It's an old music studio trick to deaden the sound—it works wonders and doesn't look half bad.

5.
The
Garage

I DON'T KNOW if you are aware of this or not, but architects have historically designed family homes to include a room called "the garage." From what I have heard, this room is actually supposed to *house a car*!

If you're lucky enough to have a garage, you know that it can be both a blessing and a burden. The garage can either make or break your sense of being an organized, together person. If you've got an organized, efficiently used garage, then you feel like an organization rock star. If, on the other hand, you use your garage as the secret place where things you don't want to deal with go to die, then chances are good that no matter how organized and together the rest of your life is, you will always feel a bit disorganized.

My garage is the laundry center, the pet feeding facility, the sporting goods department, a music and drum room, a workbench area with tools, and, of course, storage for the seasonal decorations, not to mention all the other crap that invades our home.

I like to approach the garage as if it were a ship. Ships always have incredibly efficient storage bays and compartments. Everything must be compartmentalized and out of the way, or the crew can't function effectively. The same goes for your garage—just because you have extra space doesn't mean you have to fill it all up!

Check out these ideas for making better use of your USS *Garage*.

TOOL AND WORKBENCH CENTER

When I first became the tinkering-dad-in-the-garage guy, I was well aware that my first acquisition would have to be a workbench. I had always wanted a workbench for cutting and soldering stuff, for no other reason than to exercise my free right to be a muttering, suburban, Homo sapiens tinker-geezer.

I knew my kids, being Stromers, would have a natural inclination toward building stuff, too. When I went out to purchase a workbench, I realized they all came in standard sizing that didn't suit my space. That's when I created the super-sturdy Stromer Workbench. It's cheap and easy . . . much like me after a glass of Pinot Noir. *Just saying . . .*

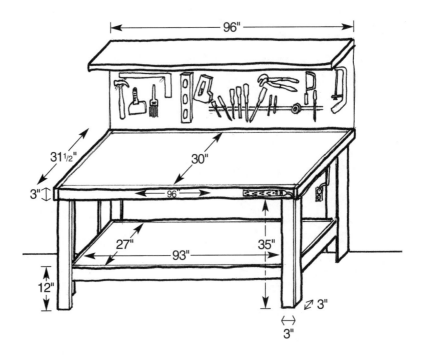

2 sheets of plywood, ¾" thick

1 box of 2" nails

1 gallon of primer (optional, if painting)

Latex paint (color of your choice)

Carpenter's glue

Three 8" shelf brackets

Drywall anchors and accompanying screws

TOOLS

Tape measure

Circular saw or table saw

Safety glasses

Hammer or nail gun and compressor

Paint tray

Paintbrushes

Stir sticks

Glass of Pinot Noir if older than 21

INSTRUCTIONS

1. Transfer the cutout lines onto your first sheet of plywood as shown on the next page, and label the pieces 1 through 11.

Workbench and Laundry Station
template 1

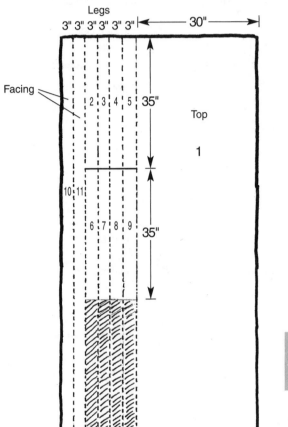

Legs

3" 3" 3" 3" 3" 3" |← —— 30" —— →|

Facing

2 | 3 | 4 | 5 | 35"

Top

1

10 | 11

6 | 7 | 8 | 9 | 35"

Denotes
scrap

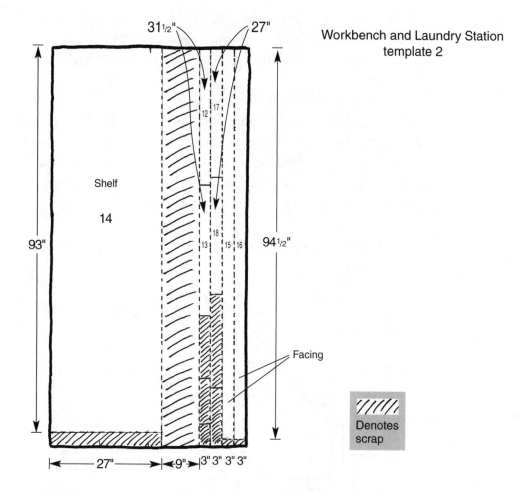

Workbench and Laundry Station
template 2

Shelf

14

93"

94½"

31½"   27"

12   17

18

13   15   16

Facing

Denotes
scrap

27"   9"   3" 3" 3" 3"

2. Transfer the cutout lines onto your second sheet of plywood as shown. Label these pieces 12 through 18.

3. For this step you will glue and nail facing pieces along all sides of the bench top. Take piece 1 (the top) and run a bead of glue along the full 8' side. Line up piece 10 (front facing) and nail it in place. Space your nails every 12" along this length. Next, glue and nail piece 11 to the other 8' side. Then proceed to install the end pieces 12 and 13, glue and nail those to the 30" sides to create a flush edge all the way around. Set the top aside for the moment.

4. To create the support shelf, locate piece 14, glue along the 27" side, and nail piece 17 to it. Repeat this step with piece 18.

5. Run a bead of glue along the 8' side and nail piece 15. Repeat with facing piece 16.

6. Set aside; it's time to assemble the legs.

7. To complete the leg assembly, take pieces 2 and 3, then glue and nail. Repeat this step with pieces 4 and 5, 6 and 7, 8 and 9. You will now have four assembled legs. Measure from the bottom of each leg up 12", and make a mark with your pencil on both the inside and outside of the assembled legs. Do this for each leg.

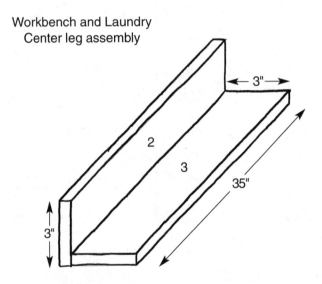

Workbench and Laundry
Center leg assembly

8. Locate the support shelf (piece 14). The flat area is the top part of the shelf. To keep from getting confused, pencil the word "top" on this section. (The overhang of the shelf points toward the floor.) Turn this piece on its side. Take one leg assembly and glue along your pencil mark on the inside of the leg and spread the glue down 3". Position the leg assembly over one corner. The longer side of the leg is positioned toward the top of the shelf. (The shorter side of the leg is positioned toward the bottom.) Nail it in place.

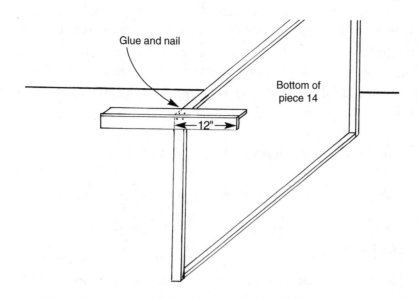

Glue and nail

Bottom of
piece 14

←—12"—→

9. Flip this piece over and attach the legs to the other side. Glue and nail them in place.

10. Set the piece upright, and set the top (piece 1) in place. In this position the legs are inset. Nail down through the top into the leg, using at least four nails in an L-shaped configuration. Repeat this procedure for the other three sets of legs.

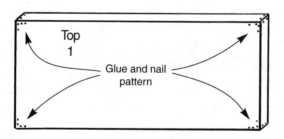

Top
1

Glue and nail
pattern

11. Now climb up on top of the table and jump up and down and marvel at the simplicity and strength of this simple two-plywood sheet table.

12. With your scrap 9" x 8' piece, make a shelf and install it with the brackets above your workbench/laundry table. See steps 18 to 21

of Home Workstation on page 139 for bracket placement and installation tips.

13. If you are limited by space and need a table less than 8' wide, simply cut down the dimensions of your plywood to suit your specific needs.

Tool and Workbench Shortcut: Under Threes

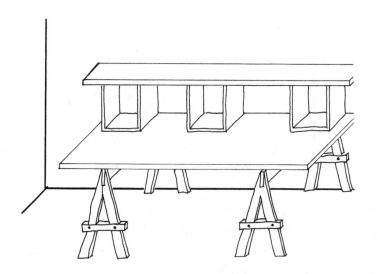

1. Arrange the sawhorses up against the wall, spaced about 4' apart.
2. Lay the door across the sawhorses.
3. For a second tier of shelving, arrange the three milk crates on top of the door. Space them evenly against the wall.
4. Locate the 1' x 12' piece of pine board and lay it across the top of the milk crates. *Voilà!* Instant workbench!

LAUNDRY CENTER

My father, the incredible Erv Stromer, spent (what must have been) eighteen years of my first eighteen years at home in the basement, doing laundry. As a family, we knew he needed this time to decompress after a long day of hocking fine French Impressionist art. In other words, I never had to do laundry as a kid.

Only after I became a parent did I realize the pressing need for a well-ordered laundry center: the quiet hum of the dryer, the tranquil sounds of swirling water filling up for the second rinse cycle. How effectively those peaceful sounds drown out the usual family utterances of "It's my ball! Mom, he took my ball! My ball . . . my ball!" Not to mention dog barking, hair-pulling, loud music by Usher screaming, *"Caught up, caught up . . . I don't know what it is but it seems she's got me twisted"*; and my wife, politely inquiring as to my whereabouts in a slightly agitated and raised tone. . . .

Me . . . with the pleasant look of a man touched by angels, looking slightly moronic and thinking: *Boy, I love this laundry center. It's so efficient and easy to keep track of things, thanks to the brilliantly designed and inexpensive laundry folding table. It's no wonder my dad spent so much time doing laundry.*

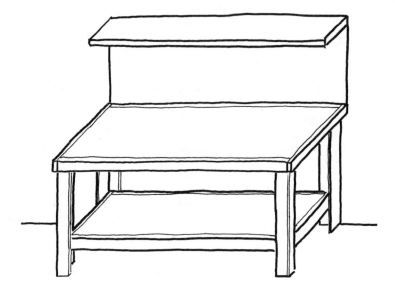

The laundry center is the exact same design as the workbench but shorter—half the length, around 4' long. Follow the directions for the workbench but cut the length dimensions in half. So instead of 8' x 30", make it 4' x 30". Also, cut your shelf down to 4' and use your off-cut to hang another 4' shelf above that one. You'll need three additional 8" shelf brackets. Now isn't that *easy?????*

PET-FOOD CADDY

The Stromers have a cat, a dog, a bearded dragon lizard, assorted fish, all sorts of woodland animals (including but not limited to raccoons), and ants, all constantly vying for a free moment in some other animal's food bowl. Plus, because of our doggy door, I was constantly finding non-Stromer-related varmints trying to eat the pet food pellets right through the bags! One day I decided I had to *stop the madness*. I got smart, and invested in 5-gallon plastic buckets with screw-on lids. And, guess what? No more varmints muscling in on my pet chow. That's when I designed my Pet-Food Caddy.

This amazing pet food center has a convenient storage box to house your pet food, treats, or kitty litter. And best of all, it can be customized to fit your personal pet needs. For example, if you only have a dog, the following half-size construction will best suit your needs. Don't forget: you don't need to locate this little baby in the garage. It's cool enough for your laundry room, utility room, basement, or even the pet area of your kitchen.

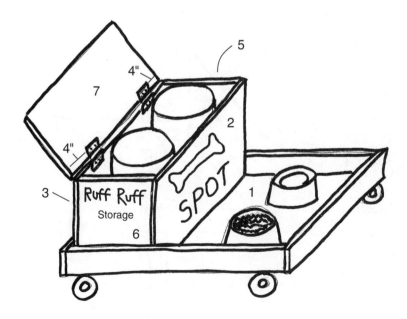

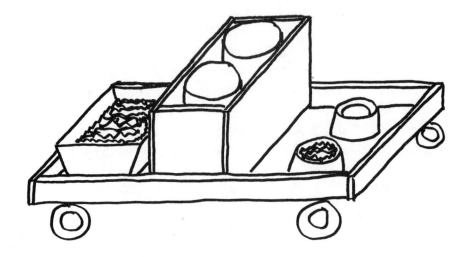

If you only have a cat, a wider full-size construction will accommodate eating tray, food storage, and litter box as well.

If you have a cat and a dog, build the low Pet-Food Caddy on wheels and the high Pet-Food Caddy on legs.

Kitty Cat Pet-Food Caddy

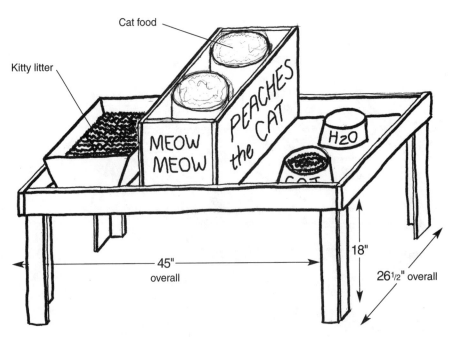

MATERIALS LIST

- 1 sheet of plywood, 3/4" thick
- Carpenter's glue
- 1 box of 1½" nails
- Two 1" wide hinges
- Primer and latex paint
- Sandpaper
- 4 small casters
- Two 5-gallon buckets with lids
- Indelible black marker

TOOLS

- Circular saw or table saw
- Safety glasses
- Hammer or nail gun and compressor
- Power drill/screwdriver
- Paintbrush

INSTRUCTIONS

1. Decide which size Pet-Food Caddy you want to build and follow the cut sheet diagram by transferring all the cut lines to your sheet of plywood. Cut them out and label them 1 through 11, as shown.

Full-size Pet-Food Caddy template

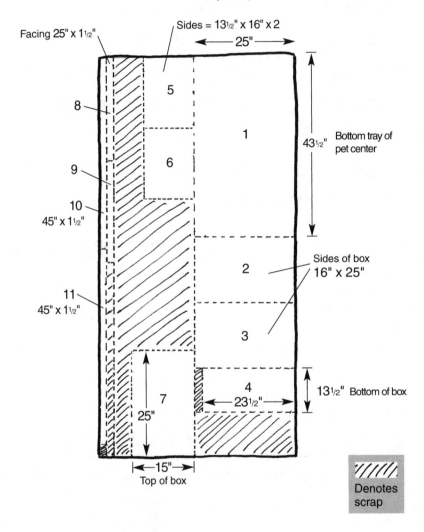

Facing 25" x 1½"

Sides = 13½" x 16" x 2

25"

8

5

1

43½" Bottom tray of pet center

9

6

10
45" x 1½"

Sides of box
16" x 25"

2

11
45" x 1½"

3

4

13½" Bottom of box

23½"

7

25"

15"

Top of box

Denotes scrap

Full-size Pet-Food Caddy with Legs template

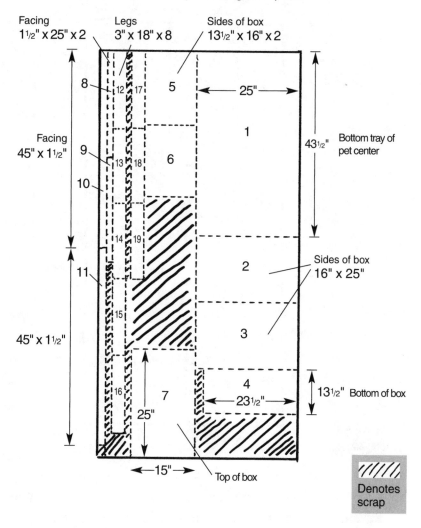

Facing
1½" x 25" x 2

Legs
3" x 18" x 8

Sides of box
13½" x 16" x 2

8

12 17   5

Facing
45" x 1½"

9

13 18   6

10

25"

Bottom tray of
pet center

43½"

1

14 19

11

45" x 1½"

15

2

Sides of box
16" x 25"

3

16   7

4

13½" Bottom of box

23½"

25"

15"   Top of box

////
Denotes
scrap

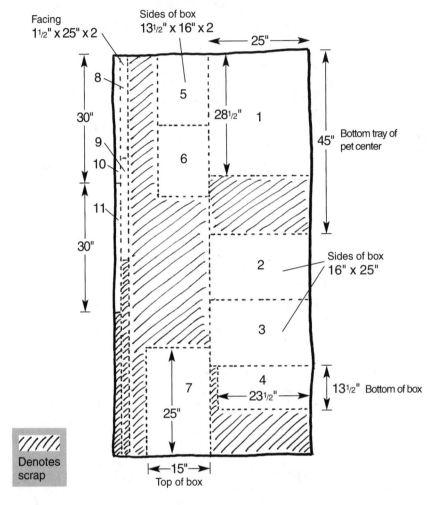

Half-size Pet-Food Caddy template

Facing
1½" x 25" x 2

Sides of box
13½" x 16" x 2

25"

8

5

30"

28½"   1

45" Bottom tray of
pet center

9

10

6

11

30"

2

Sides of box
16" x 25"

3

7

4
23½"

13½" Bottom of box

25"

/////
Denotes
scrap

←15"→
Top of box

2. Locate piece 1 (which is the top) and run a bead of glue along the 25" side and nail piece 8 (facing) to it. Use four nails evenly spaced. Repeat on the other 25" side, using facing piece 9. Locate pieces 10 and 11, and proceed to glue and nail them in order to complete installation of the facing. Follow one of these two illustrations for construction, depending on whether you are making the half-size tray or the full-size tray. Set this part aside.

Half-size base for Pet-Food Caddy

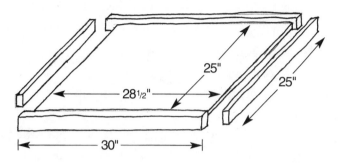

25"

28½"

25"

30"

Full-size base for Pet-Food Caddy

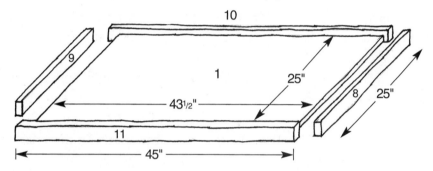

10

9

1

25"

25"

43½"

8

11

45"

3. To construct the food storage box, locate long side pieces 2 and 3 and short side pieces 5 and 6 and the bottom piece 4. Line up pieces 2 and 5 into a right angle (piece 5 forms the outside edge). Nail together every 4".

Food and Litter storage box

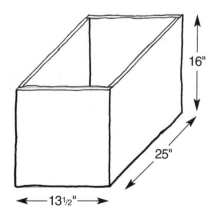

16"

25"

13½"

4. Slide the bottom piece into this right angle and nail in place along the edge, every 4".

5. Repeat right angle assembly with pieces 3 and 6, then attach to unit to create a box. First nail along the lower edge. Then nail through the end pieces to complete the sides.

6. Flip the box upright and lay piece 7 on top to dry fit it for your hinge placement.

7. Open the top as if it were hinged and pencil mark the placement of your hinges 4" in from either end of the lid. (Refer to the Pet-Food Caddy on page 157 for hinge placement.)

8. Pre-drill, with a slightly smaller drill bit, right on those hole markings. Be careful not to drill through the other side. Use the old tape-on-the-bit trick as a depth plunge gauge (see page 129).

9. Screw in your hinges.

10. Grab your Pet-Food Caddy tray and find dead center on the 43^1/$_2$" side (or 28^1/$_2$"); draw a line across the short side of the tray at this point. This line will indicate the placement of your food storage box.

11. Next, measure to the left 13^1/$_2$" and draw a line on that mark as well.

Note: Most drill/screwdrivers have a variable speed trigger. When driving very short screws, it's important to learn the fine art of easing your trigger so that the screw rotates slowly, yet still maintaining pressure on the screw as it goes into the wood. If you don't ease the trigger of the drill/screwdriver, you run the risk of rotating the screw too quickly and stripping the head. Stripping the head means that the slots which the tip of the screwdriver locks can no longer be turned. If this does occur, you will need to use a pair of pliers to manually remove the screw and replace with a new one. Practice makes perfect.

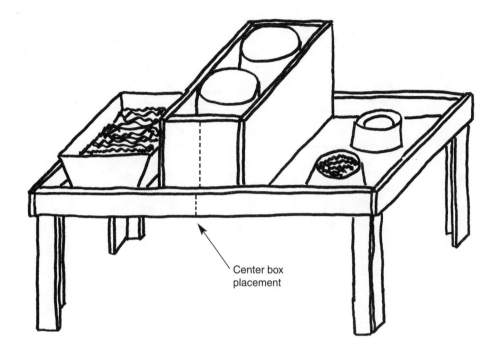

Center box
placement

12. Grab the storage box with lid, which you assembled earlier. Spread a fair amount of glue on the bottom of the box. When gluing a large area like the bottom of a box, I like to write the names of my family in glue. Or the concentric circle method works well, too. Think of it like decorating a cake!

13. Flip the box back over and line it up with that line you just drew 13½" off center. This will place the box right in the center of the tray.

14. Flip the whole thing on its side and install your casters 1½" from the sides in all four corners. Make sure your caster screws don't exceed ¾" or the screw heads will poke through the tray.

For the Pet Center with Legs, locate leg pieces 12 through 19. Assemble two pieces together to make a right angle as shown on page 152 (Leg assembly for workbench). Create four legs. To attach the legs, turn the Pet Food Center upside down. Position the legs into each corner and nail through the facing on each side. Then turn the Pet Food Center over and nail down through the top on each side of each leg.

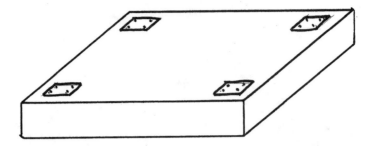

15. Flip the unit upright and prime. Sketch your pets' names on the outside of the box. Be creative and make any designs you think your pets would like! Trace over with an indelible black marker and fill in with your paint colors of choice.

16. Open your lid and fill up your two 5-gallon buckets with whatever you want. Put your pets' food and water bowls on one side and your cat litter box on the other and watch the magic happen!

Pet-Food Caddy Shortcut: Under Threes

MATERIALS	
1 or 2 plastic or wood milk crates	A collection of well-sealed containers for food storage
1 whisk broom and dustpan	

The most valuable shortcut I can offer for this project would be to suggest that you invest in a whisk broom and dustpan for permanent storage nearby. Use this convenient tool to keep this area clean and free of stray kibble and partially chewed wet food. As you know, stray kibble will attract varmints and lead to waste. I also think keeping this area clean is a great chore for children from the age of five and up. This is something they can expect to do to earn the right to have a pet in the first place.

Once you have a clean, secure area, the idea is to keep it that way. Assemble a collection of well-sealed containers for storing the food and treats. When you're trying to keep your garage together, there is nothing worse than an out-of-control pet food center.

I-DON'T-HAVE-TO-BE-PSYCHIC SPORTS WALL

The kids have been in the house too long. They're crazy and need to exercise. You've finally coaxed them to go outside and play basketball . . . but wait! The unthinkable has happened. They can't find their basketball. They can't even find a tennis ball. The window of opportunity has passed and the kids have all gone back inside as you mutter to yourself, "Where is that basketball? I know I put it here somewhere. . . ."

This was the bane of my existence until I designed the I-Don't-Have-to-Be-Psychic Sports Wall. With just a few open feet of wall space in your garage and some creative wood peg and hanging devices, your garage will actually *help you* in taking advantage of future opportunities to get your kids *out of the darn house, darn it.*

- One 1" x 6" x 8' piece of pine
- 8' length of 1/4" dowel
- 4" screws (if drilling into studs; if not, use 4 drywall anchors)
- Carpenter's glue
- Mesh ball bags available at sporting goods stores with drawstring openings
- All the balls, bats, rackets, lacrosse sticks, or Frisbees you haven't been able to find

TOOLS

- Chop saw
- Safety glasses
- Power drill/screwdriver
- 1/4" drill bit
- Pencil and straightedge
- Tape measure
- Hammer

INSTRUCTIONS

1. Using a pencil and straightedge, draw a line straight down the center from top to bottom on the 1" x 6" piece of pine. The 8' length of this board will be the width of your sports wall.

Note: If you don't have 8' of wall space or if you don't need a full 8' of storage, you can cut your piece of pine down to the appropriate length.

2. Lay out your tape measure along this line and make a mark every 4".

3. Fit your drill with a 1/4" drill bit and drill a hole straight through at each mark every 4".

4. Locate your ¹/₄" dowel and cut it into pieces 5" long. For an 8' wide sports wall, with dowels every 4", you will need 19 dowel pieces.

5. Lay your 8' piece of pine down flat on its back.

6. Pour out a puddle of carpenter's glue on a paper plate or some newspaper.

7. Take your 5" lengths and dip them in the glue to about 3/4" up the dowel.

8. Insert the end with glue into each hole and tap in lightly with a hammer to set the dowel in place.

9. Find a spot on the wall of your garage and install either right into the studs every 16" or use drywall anchors. If you use drywall anchors, pre-drill holes at both ends of the 8' length and two more holes centered in the middle.

10. Make a pencil mark through the holes and onto the drywall. Remove your board and drill drywall anchors right into those pencil marks. Put the board back up, fitting over the drywall anchors and screw into place until the unit fits snug against the wall.

11. Fill up your mesh bags with sporting goods and don't ever tell me you can't find your sports stuff again.

Now that you've got the world's most awesome garage, check out these tips for keeping it that way.

ERIC'S FIVE BEST IDEAS FOR A CLEAN AND ORGANIZED GARAGE

1. **Wrangle your stuff.** Set boundaries for your gear. Keep each type of item in a specific, designated area. Think of how your kids never want different food items to touch on their plate. Behave the same way regarding your garage floor and shelving. Ewww, the yucky laundry basket found its way over to the workshop area. . . . *Mom!*

2. **Build shelves.** Use all open wall space for shelving or display. If I'm ever invited to any of your homes to see a play on your stage or have some scrumptious meat loaf, I'd better not see any empty walls in your garage! Because our goal is *to keep the floor empty of all boxes and clutter.* Always use all wall space to store or warehouse your garage-bound belongings.

3. **Watch your overhead.** Don't forget the ceiling. Whenever possible, get your boats, bicycles, airplanes, whatever up off the floor and securely fasten stuff to garage ceiling framing. You don't ever see cluttered aisles in warehouses. It would prevent workers from accessing their inventory. You need to handle *your* inventory the same way.

4. **Honor the car.** Keep an open area in the middle of your garage for your car . . . even if you don't park there. It's good garage clutter-management psychology! Just the act of creating a boundary in the center of your garage will keep you from losing control of your space.

5. **Use it or . . . or lose it.** Don't keep unused stuff. It's the same principle as the outdated clothes in your closet. If you find you're no longer using that plastic kiddy slide from when your daughter was three, get rid of it! Now that she's graduating from college and entering the job market, I doubt she'll have use for it.

6.
The
Backyard

IF PROPERLY ORGANIZED, your backyard can double the usable living space of your home, weather permitting. That means one thing and one thing only: inner peace and tranquillity because your kids are outside, occupied in a safe and fun place, and you are *not*!

You *can* still keep an eye on them, but you can also sit inside and keep waving as you have your first uninterrupted phone call (*"Dusty, put down the anvil!"*) since your kids developed their own personalities, the stinkers.

My goal for *your* backyard is to make it a playground, a family game area, and a place to admire your beautiful garden while marveling at one child's ability to use the skateboard ramp that *he* built, as the other one quietly plays Bowlquet in your very own outdoor game area. All within complete privacy, because your new fence extension is so efficient your neighbor can't possibly see you secretly napping in the teepee you built with your kids. That's not too much to ask from your backyard, is it?

YOUR DREAM SANDBOX

I swear my kids were desert nomads in a past life. They both took to the sandbox so quickly—I guess there's just something about filling up buckets with sand and then dumping them out over and over again that my kids can't live without. This a great first project to help you and the family buff up your do-it-yourself skills and build some confidence to tackle more complicated projects.

WARNING! Never use pressure-treated wood for any play structures! It contains arsenic and other toxic chemicals, which is why it doesn't rot.

MATERIALS LIST

- Two 2" x 8" x 8' redwood or cedar pieces of wood (Douglas fir is O.K., but you should know it will rot faster)

- 1 roll of 6 millilambers (or thicker) plastic

- 10 bags of play sand

- 1 half sheet of plywood, ½" thick

- 1 box of 3" galvanized nails or, even better, 3" deck screws

- Primer and paint if you're using Douglas fir or painting the sandbox lid (If you use redwood or cedar, don't paint or stain the wood. They naturally hold up to weather much better without any products on them.)

- Tons of sandbox toys

TOOLS

- Circular saw or handsaw (Precision is not so crucial with this project.)

- Safety glasses

- Power drill/screwdriver

- Staple gun and staples

- Hammer or screw gun

- Tape measure

1. The sandbox is a basic box construction. Begin by cutting the two 8" x 8' pieces of redwood in half to make four 8" x 4' pieces of redwood.

2. Create a right angle with two of the 4' lengths and nail or screw together.

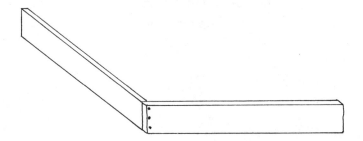

3. Do the same with the other two pieces of 4'-long wood. Then attach the two L-shape pieces together with nails or wood screws. You will have created a 4' x 4' square.

4. Move the square to the desired location in your backyard. Use the staple gun to line the inside of the square with the plastic sheeting. Attach the sheeting 2" from the top edge, with a staple approximately every 2". Dump in your bags of sand. Woo-hoo!

5. To create the top, locate your plywood and cut it down the middle. You will now have two 2' x 4' pieces, which are more manageable to lift off and put back on. You may want to drill a 1/2" finger hole in the center of the long edge of each piece to make it easier to grasp and pull.

6. If desired, prime and paint the lid with flowers, bees, ladybugs, butterflies, castles, or anything else you always dreamed you would have as a kid but never got.

7. Dump in your sand toys and invite the neighborhood.

When the kids have finished playing, put the lid back on, particularly in cat-friendly areas.

PEEWEE TEEPEE

What could be better than your own teepee? I'll tell you what—
NOTHING! I'll never forget the first time I ever went inside a teepee. I
was crossing the great prairie with nothing but a buckskin knife and
some beef jerky. I must have been no older than ten. A steady, hard
rain came down in torrents. Thank goodness I was near the hardware
store and could purchase all the materials I needed to make my first
Peewee Teepee. You'd better shop now, too.

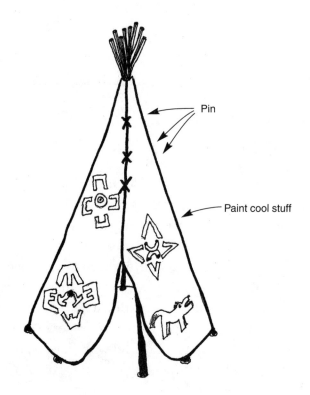

Pin

Paint cool stuff

MATERIALS LIST

  Eight ¾" x 6' bamboo poles

 A 9' x 12' canvas painter's tarp

 6 large safety pins (Diaper pins are not only the right size, they are also safe.)

  A 45' x ⅛" clothesline

 Acrylic craft paint in an assortment of colors

TOOLS

 Scissors

Tape measure

 Paintbrush

Safety glasses

INSTRUCTIONS

1. Cut one 4' piece of clothesline and lash together three of your bamboo poles, 8" from the top, to form a tripod. Spread the poles approximately 5' apart around an imaginary circle.

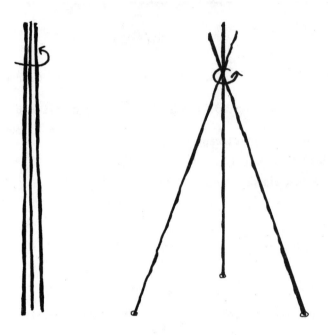

2. Interlace the remaining five poles so they are approximately 2'
apart from each other around the same imaginary circle.

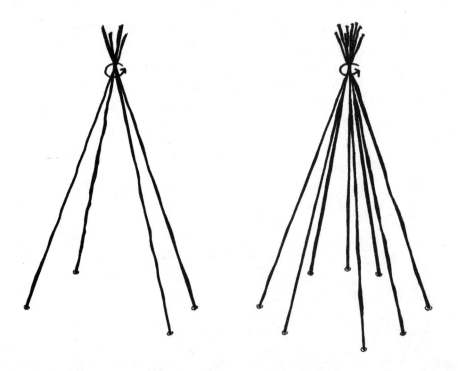

3. Cut a 4' length of clothesline and tie it to one pole, then walk around your teepee, wrapping the clothesline around the bamboo poles until you get near the end of your line. Tie the line off so it's tight around all eight poles.

4. You now have your teepee frame. If erecting this masterpiece outside on the lawn, you can lightly tap the top of all eight bamboo poles to gently drive the ends down into the soil.

5. Now locate the 9' x 12' tarp. You are going to cut off 3' from the long end, making the tarp a 9' x 9' square. An easy way to do this is to simply grab one corner and fold it across to the other side, creating a 45-degree triangle. The excess part of the canvas will equal 3'. Go ahead and use your scissors to cut it off.

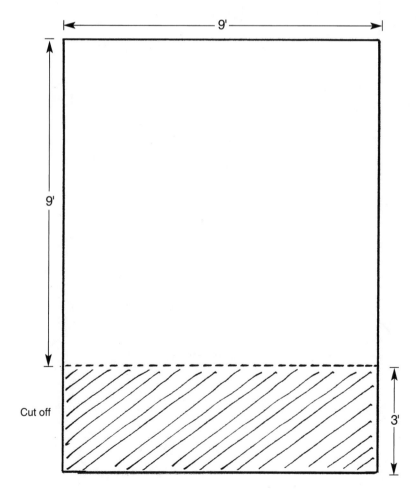

Denotes scrap

6. Continue to fold this triangle four more times, creating smaller triangles each time.

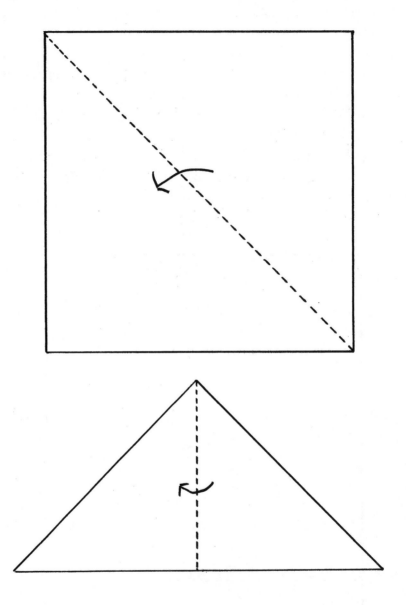

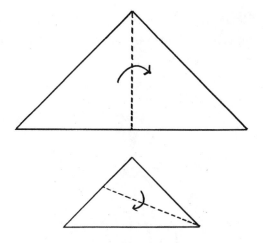

7. Use the scissors to make a cut as shown.

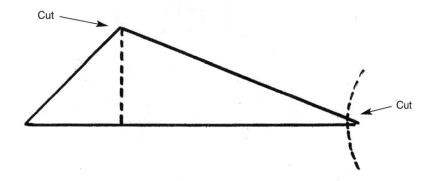

8. When you unfold your tarp, it should look more or less like a poncho.

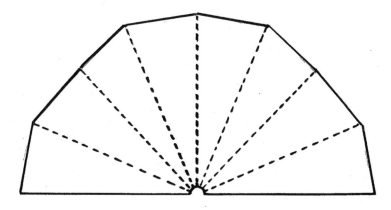

9. Drape the tarp around the bamboo poles. Use the large safety pins to secure the fabric around the poles and hold it together at the entrance point. You will leave a 3' entrance slit open.

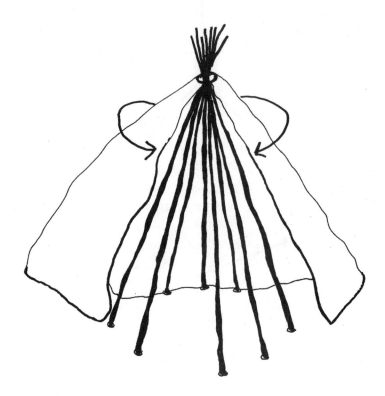

10. Your Peewee Teepee is now ready for you to decorate with symbols of your tribe. If you like, you may use the ones designed by my seven-year-old son, "Running Haywire Wyatt," as your inspiration.

LIGHTNING

SUN

WYATT STROMER

EARTH

NIGHT

STORM

TIME

ULTIMATE SKATEBOARD RAMP

I love skateboarding. I think it's a great way to learn about balance. Unfortunately, it is also completely crazy unless full pads (knee, elbow, wrist, hand guards, and especially a helmet!) are used. Once your kid makes it past the initial learning curve, they'll want to take a few more risks.

In other words, skateboarding can make Mom's and Dad's heart go pitter-patter and not in a good way. My skateboard ramps are well constructed and keep the "danger" at home, under a watchful eye. My ramp design also allows for the three sections to be easily broken down and stored in your lean and organized garage.

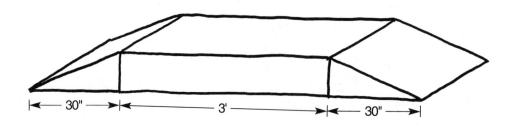

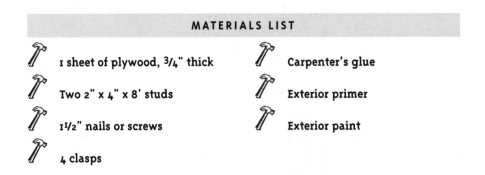

MATERIALS LIST	
1 sheet of plywood, 3/4" thick	Carpenter's glue
Two 2" x 4" x 8' studs	Exterior primer
1¹/2" nails or screws	Exterior paint
4 clasps	

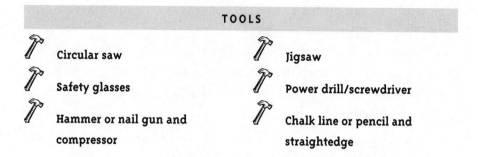

TOOLS

🔨 Circular saw

🔨 Safety glasses

🔨 Hammer or nail gun and
compressor

🔨 Jigsaw

🔨 Power drill/screwdriver

🔨 Chalk line or pencil and
straightedge

INSTRUCTIONS

1. Transfer the cutting lines from the diagram to your plywood.

Skateboard Ramp template

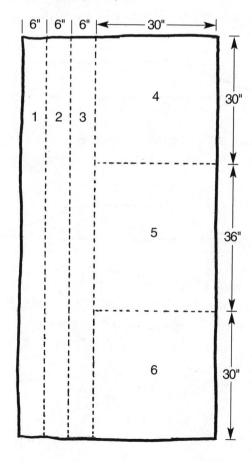

2. Number the pieces 1 through 6 as shown in the diagram. Go ahead and cut out all your pieces.

3. Lay out piece 1 horizontally. Measure in from the left and make a mark at 30" with your chalk line or straightedge. Then make a line from that point back toward your lower, left corner, creating a triangle. Cut along the angle.

Skateboard Ramp angle cut template

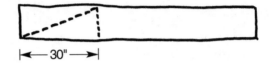

|←— 30" —→|

4. Repeat on the other end. Cut this piece off as well. Reserve the off-cut angles, as you will need them in a few minutes.

5. Use the newly shaped piece 1, as shown, as a template and lay it over piece 2. Transfer the off-cut shapes onto 2 and repeat onto 3.

6. Cut off the angles from pieces 2 and 3.

7. You will now have six angle pieces that you cut off from pieces 1, 2, and 3. Label these six angle pieces 7 through 12.

8. Locate piece 7, measure a 3^{1}/$_{2}$" x 1^{1}/$_{2}$" cutout at the 90-degree angle. Use your saw to remove this piece.

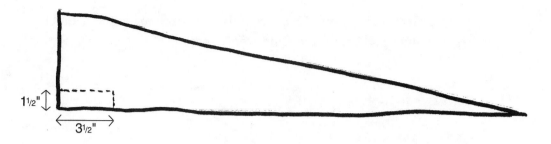

1½"

3½"

9. Use piece 7 as a template and repeat this cutout configuration on piece 8 by laying piece 7 on top of piece 8 and tracing the cutout.

10. You should now have pieces 7 and 8 with the 3½" x 1½" cutout of them and pieces 9 through 12 as whole angles with no cutouts.

11. Locate a 2" x 4" stud and measure three sections of 28½" pieces. Then, cut a fourth 28½" section from the other 2" x 4" x 8' stud. You should now have four 28½" pieces.

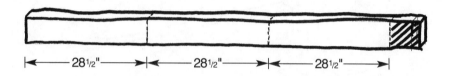

28½"   28½"   28½"

12. Locate piece 1 and, using a jigsaw, cut out two 3½" notches from either end, measuring 1½" deep.

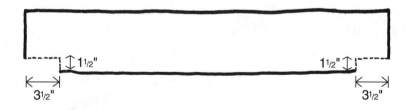

1½"   1½"

3½"   3½"

13. You are now ready to assemble.

14. Grab one of your 2" x 4" sections and attach to piece 9. Don't forget to glue! Nail with three nails evenly spaced.

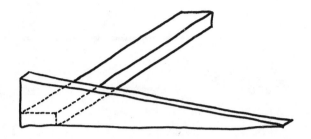

15. Locate piece 7. Measure along the 2" x 4" section to 14¼". Glue along that line and around the side and nail from underneath up into the piece.

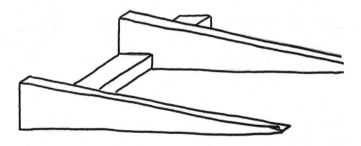

16. Next, locate piece 10 and attach, with glue and three nails, to the opposite end of the 2" x 4" from piece 9.

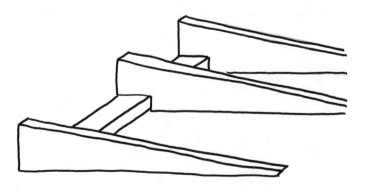

17. Repeat the same configuration with another 2" x 4" section and pieces 8, 11, and 12. These will create two ramps.

18. Now to assemble the center portion, or fun box* section of the skateboard ramp, locate the remaining two 2" x 4" pieces and nail them to pieces 1, 2, and 3.

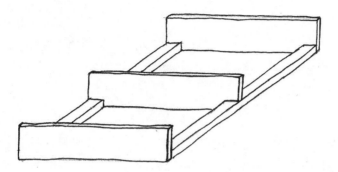

19. Locate pieces 4 and 6. Line them up on top of your ramp constructions. Use glue and nails up each ramp every 6". Make sure you also glue and nail the center support rail, as well.

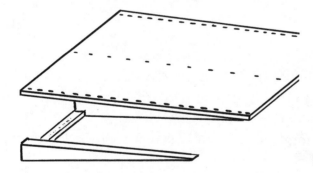

Note: You want to take care to hammer every nail straight in, and leave no nail head sticking up, as this will interfere with smooth skateboarding and will be a hazard to tender kiddy skin and noggins.

*The fun box is a skater term for the flat rectangle section.

20. Lay piece 5 on top of the platform framing, line up the edges and corners. Secure in place with nails and glue.

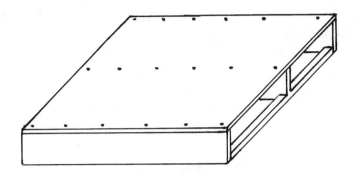

21. Install a clasp on both sides of both skateboard ramps to enable you to "lock" them together with the platform so they won't move while you are using them.

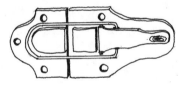

22. Prime and paint your ramps with any design you like. I love making the ramps look like a racetrack with a broken center.

23. When your kids are finished using the ramp, you can easily break it down into three easy-to-store pieces.

24. Don't forget to tell your kids how cool Uncle Eric says their safety gear is!

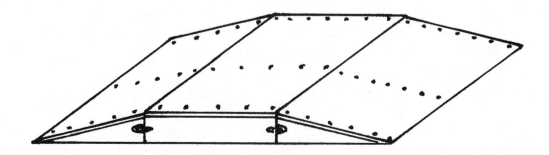

I have a neighbor who loves to enjoy his hot tub . . . in his *Speedo*. Help! It's not just his fashion sense, it's his back hair and gut that make me nervous. Then, one crisp October evening, he burst out his door with just a cowboy hat and a beer, singing "Love Me Tender." *That's it,* I thought, *I'm making my fence higher!*

A little 2' x 4' framework and some redwood lattice and you're back to privacy in no time. My fence extension is assembled in 8' x 1' sections and can be easily removed at any time. Who knows, maybe after Speedo guy finally sells, there will be someone we'll want to see playing naked bocce ball!

I'll show you how to construct one 8' section and you simply multiply that by the number of linear feet you require to top off all of your fencing. You might also ask your local nursery which vines thrive in your climate. Plant some tall stuff to get into that latticework and really obscure the view.

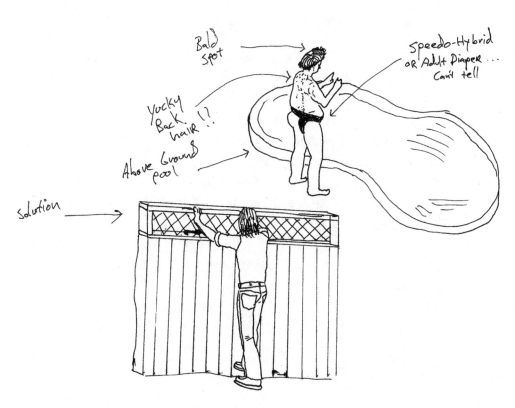

(Makes one 8' x 1' section)

- Three 2" x 4" x 8' redwood or cedar studs
- 1 box of 3" deck screws or nails
- 1" deck screws or nails
- A sheet of redwood lattice (4' x 8')

TOOLS

- Circular saw
- Safety glasses
- Power drill/screwdriver
- Hammer or screw gun
- Tape measure
- Chalk line

INSTRUCTIONS

1. Cut one of the 2" x 4" studs into four 2' sections. Set aside.
2. Use the chalk line to mark the lattice into equal halves, 2' x 8'.
3. Cut along this line with the circular saw.
4. Lay out the pieces as shown. The two full studs create the top and bottom. The 2' stud pieces align on each end and one is placed directly in the center of the fence section.
5. Use the 3" deck screws or nails to fasten the studs together.
6. Lay half of the lattice sheet over the stud frame and use the 1" nails to fasten it in place.
7. To install this section to extend the height of your fence, you will need to nail down through the bottom of a 2" x 4" stud into your existing fence.

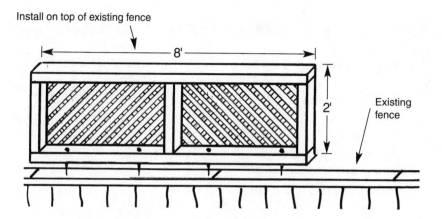

Install on top of existing fence

8'

2'

Existing fence

8. Sing along with Eric . . . Ready? Begin: "No more Speedo . . . no more back hair . . . end of bald spot . . . yard free of despair . . ."

SIMPLE, ONE-DAY STONE PATIO

Want to build a Simple, One-Day Stone Patio? While planning for my son's seventh birthday party, I needed a dance floor for break-dancers, but first I was going to need a flat area that would support the dance-floor panels. And before I knew it, *bam!* I was engaged in a patio-building project I had put off for months. As it turns out, children's looming birthday parties are the *true* mother of invention.

This simple patio I devised measures 9' x 12', or approximately 108 square feet. Any larger and I would have to call it the Exhausting, *Two-*Day Stone Patio.

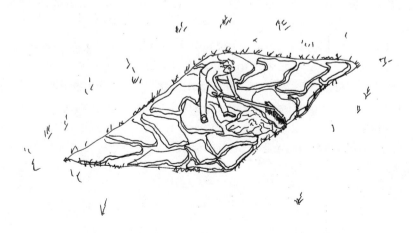

MATERIALS LIST

 Stone or pavers to fill 9' x 12'

 Sand to cover 9' x 12' (to cover base 1" thick)

 Decomposed granite (also known as DG) to fill 3/4" to 1" grout joints for a 9' x 12' area

 2 sheets of plywood, 1/4" thick

 Can of spray paint, any color (ideally something you have left over from another project)

TOOLS

Tape measure

Hammer

Spade or shovel

Stone chisel

Safety glasses

Push broom

At a stone yard or building supply store, tell the salesperson you need to fill a 9' x 12' area with the stone of your choice. Ask to see the outdoor stone selection and try to pick stones that are all fairly close in thickness. For best results, choose stones with a thickness of 3/4" or more. If you'd like a more tailored look, this plan will work just as well with 12" x 12" x 1" or 16" x 16" x 1" pavers. Ask your salesperson how much DG you'll need to fill in 3/4" to 1" grout joints for a 9' x 12' area.

I recommend that you have the stone, sand, and DG delivered, unless you want to rent a pickup and do *a lot* of shoveling. Besides, it's better that you save your strength for setting the stones and grouting. Hire other people to wheelbarrow all the stuff to your patio site. Or bribe your neighbors with delicious hamburgers and hot dogs to be cooked right there on your new patio that they helped you create. *Go team!*

STROMER SLICK TIP: Have the sand dumped on a sheet of plywood next to your work area, and the DG on a separate plywood sheet. You want to keep them separate and on the plywood because this stuff is really hard to get out of the grass and will create dead spots.

You will fill in the space between the stones (grout lines) with the decomposed granite. I use DG because all you have to do is shovel it on the stones once they're in place and sweep the DG back and forth across the stone forcing it into all the cracks. Hose it down and keep sweeping it into the cracks until the DG is level with the top of the stone.

INSTRUCTIONS

1. Measure out a 9' x 12' area in your yard. You can easily mark this area by spraying a thin stripe of spray paint onto the grass. (You will be digging it up anyway.)

2. Prep your patio area by removing grass. Use a shovel, preferably a spade, and create a 9' x 12' rectangle by digging up a perimeter line where you intend to lay your stone. Be watchful of sprinkler heads and sprinkler lines. Only dig down about 2" or just enough to remove the top layer of grass. Discard grass and dirt.

Note: In some areas you may need to rent a Dumpster to haul away this debris . . . or you could just put a handful in your pocket every time you go out, and in 300 years you will get it off your property.

STROMER SLICK TIP: To make digging easier, saturate the area with water the night before.

3. Pour sand into the area. Use a 2" x 4" to *screed* (or spread) your sand to 1" thick. I suggest using a 2" x 4" to pull the sand toward you in a gentle sawing motion, which will level the sand pretty efficiently. This layer of sand serves as the bed for the stone. Sand also does a great job of compensating for the variable thickness of the stone. If necessary, you can add or remove sand from underneath individual stones to make your patio level.

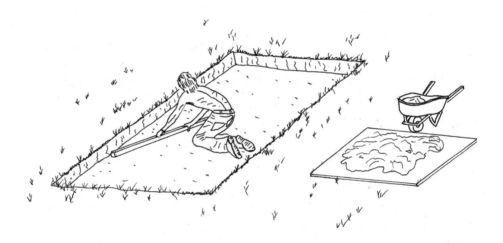

STROMER SLICK TIP: I would also suggest that you follow the lay of your land, as it already exists. Trying to make the whole area perfectly level will require too much excavating and sand and you'll rue the day you ever started. Just make it as flat as possible.

4. Lay your stones out randomly, trying to keep them 3/4" to 1" apart. Don't worry too much about arranging the stones in an orderly fashion. This patio is intended for randomly placed stones. A good general rule is to scatter all your big stones first and then fill in around them with smaller ones.

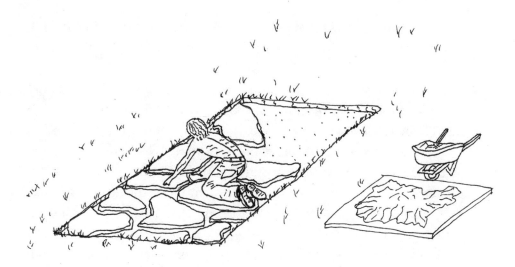

Whatever large spaces you find after setting all the bigger stones should be filled in with pieces you chip off of the medium stones.

5. To chip stone, first score with a stone chisel or gently chip a line with the claw end of a hammer.

Note: To chisel stone safely, MAKE SURE TO WEAR SAFETY GLASSES!

Try not to make the line too linear. Place the part of the stone you just scored over a straightedge like a 2" x 4" or another stone, and gently tap along the line of the piece you want with a hammer. It will break off in pieces, but that's O.K., just use what best fits in the spaces you need to fill.

6. Once the stones are in place, shovel your DG into the cracks as best you can. Let it overflow above the stone by at least 1 1/2". Pack it down by walking like a tightrope walker across the grout lines, squishing it into place with your feet. This is a great time to haul in all your kids and their friends to help you. Put on some music. Really liven this up! Get them all worked up, because the next step will really set them free.

7. Hand over the hose to your kids and have them spray the whole patio until the DG looks like a slurry of sandy mud. Then take a

push broom and sweep back and forth across the joints. Don't sweep along the joints or you'll pull out the DG that you're trying to sweep in.

8. Let the whole mess dry until the grout area looks hazy. Leave it for approximately 20 minutes, and then repeat the tightrope stomping. Fill in any low grout areas with more DG and repack.

9. Go through the watering-stomping-drying bit several times until all the DG is level with the top of the stone. Let it dry and then sweep off excess DG from the stone only. Sweep into your shovel, using it like a dustpan, and remove all excess sand and DG . . . then throw it over your fence into the neighbor's yard! *Just kidding.*

10. By now it's about 6:30 P.M. and you need to take a long bath and think to yourself, *I can't believe we just did all that! A one-day patio that would have cost us $2,500 and we did for $500. Thank God we saved $2,000. Now we can use that money to have someone haul all the extra sand out of our neighbor's yard. . . .*

"YARD-MOIRE" FOR OUTDOOR DRY STORAGE

The backyard area requires a lot of "stuff." The problem? Where to store it all? Keeping clutter at bay is the key for enjoying your home . . . even in the backyard. My Yard-Moire for Outdoor Dry Storage is a convenient way to store all of your backyard tools, games, and recreational aids in one easily accessible location.

The inside configuration of the Yard-Moire can be customized to suit your specific needs. Gardening supplies may need a taller section to hold rakes and shovels. A family with a lot of backyard toys may want more shelves. What I show here is a basic layout, so feel free to be creative.

This weather-resistant shed is a great first lesson in simple cabinet-making and is an easy enough design to include the whole family in the project. Build your own Yard-Moire and it will store, protect, and serve for years to come.

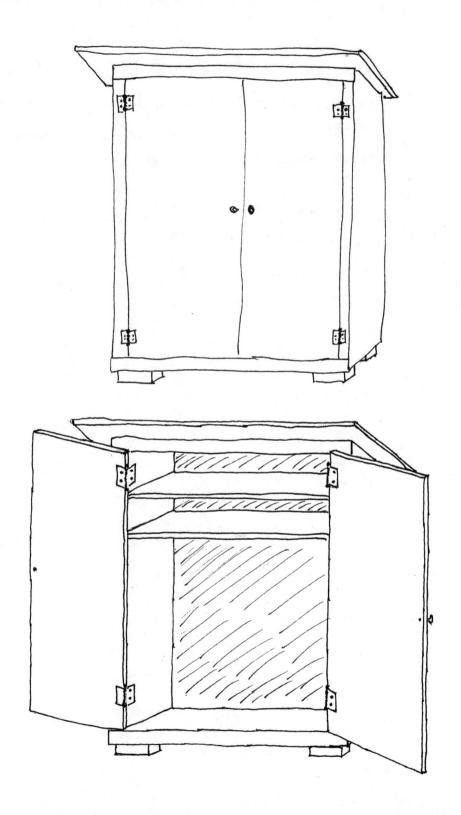

MATERIALS LIST	
3 sheets of plywood, 3/4" thick, exterior grade	A small roll of roofing material
1 sheet of plywood, 1/4" thick (for backing)	Exterior primer and exterior paint
Five 1" x 2" x 8' pieces of pine	2 door handles
Four 2" exterior hinges	2 door catches
A small box of 3/4" galvanized roofing nails	Carpenter's glue
	One box of 1 1/2" drywall screws

TOOLS	
Circular saw or table saw	Power drill/screwdriver
Safety glasses	Paintbrush or roller
Hammer or nail gun and compressor	

1. Transfer the working lines from my diagrams onto your three sheets of plywood, and label the pieces 1 through 10.

Yard-Moire Storage templates

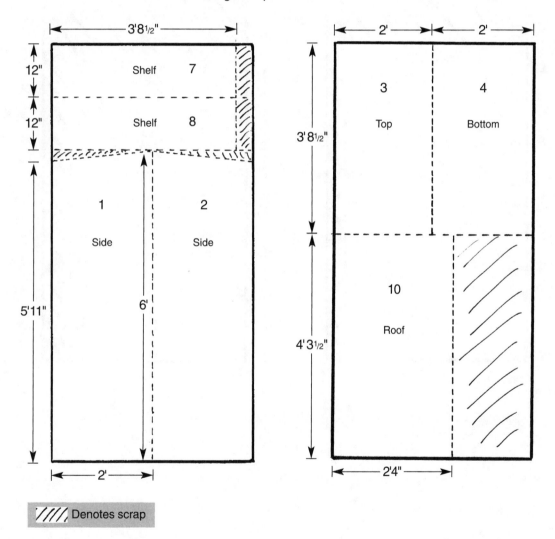

Denotes scrap

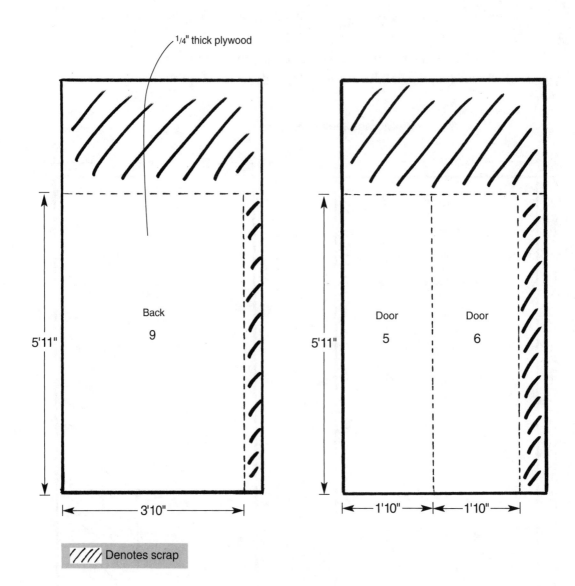

¼" thick plywood

Back
9

5'11"

3'10"

Door
5

Door
6

5'11"

1'10"

1'10"

///// Denotes scrap

2. Using glue and nails create an L-shape with pieces 1 and 4.

3. Glue and nail the top portion of piece 1 to piece 3.

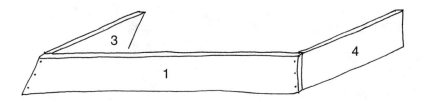

4. Glue and nail number 2, your other side piece, to complete all four sides of the Yard-Moire.

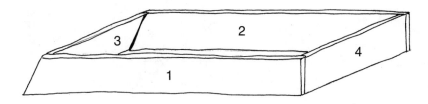

5. Measure down from point A 12³/₄" and make a mark on both sides. This is where your top shelf will be.

6. Measure down from point A 24³/₄" and make a mark on both sides. This is where your second shelf will be.

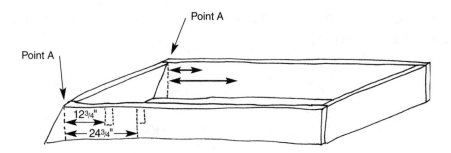

7. Glue and nail pieces 7 and 8 at those marks.

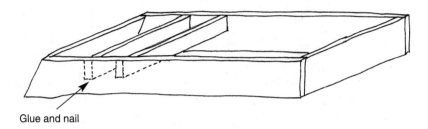

Glue and nail

8. It's time to put on the back of the Yard-Moire, folks! This is piece 9, cut from the thinner piece of plywood.

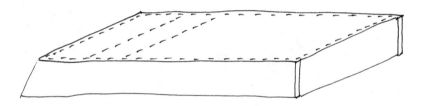

9. Glue and nail all edges of your Yard-Moire, including your shelves. Glue every 6".

10. Locate your five strips of 1" x 2" x 8' of pine. For your facing you need the following lengths: two 6' lengths, two 3'7" lengths, and two 3'8 1/2" lengths.

11. Flip your Yard-Moire over and face all of your edges with your facing. Don't forget to glue.

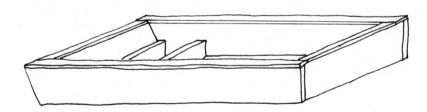

12. Measure down from point A 12" and 60" on both sides for hinge placement. Make marks.

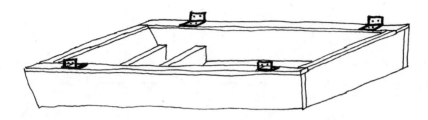

13. Have a helper or two hold pieces 5 and 6, the doors, in place so you can mark the hinge placements on the doors. Make sure you line up the doors with the top and bottom of the Yard-Moire.

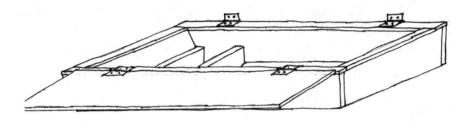

14. Take the doors away and pre-drill the cabinet doors. Make sure you don't drill through the cabinet doors!

15. From scrap plywood, cut 16 rectangular pieces, 2" x 4". Stack four together and make a glue sandwich. Shoot four nails through each one to hold it together while the glue dries. These will be the cabinet's legs.

16. It's time to screw the legs to the bottom of the Yard-Moire. You will be screwing down into the legs through the bottom of the Yard-Moire.

17. Measure 1" in from the front and the sides, and 1" in from the back and the sides. Trace your legs on the bottom like this.

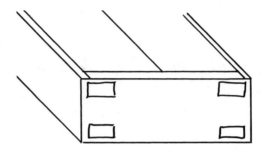

18. Glue the tops of the legs in place, and from the inside of the cabinet, pre-drill and screw four 1¹/₂" drywall screws into each leg.

19. To attach the roof piece to the top of the Yard-Moire, lay down heavy beads of glue all over the top of the unit. Take the final roof piece and lay it on top. Make sure each side has a 3" overhang and the front and back has a 2" overhang. Secure to top with three rows of screws, every 8".

20. Cut roofing material to size and cover roof with 3/4" galvanized roofing nails. Nail every 6".

21. Lift your Yard-Moire upright and install door catches on the top and bottom of the cabinet frame: *male,* or protruding, hardware on doors; *female,* or receptacle, hardware on the frame of cabinet.

22. Install handles of your choice. Prime and paint to your personal specifications.

23. Put all your yard stuff and toys inside for dry storage for hundreds of years to come. You built it; the Yard-Moire can take it!

OUTDOOR GAME AREA: BOWLQUET

Now that you want to spend so much time in your backyard, you're going to need an outdoor game area. Aside from the standard Frisbee, football, badminton, horseshoe, and baseball areas, there are some other possibilities.

Have you ever heard of Bowlquet? (Lawn bowling plus croquet equals Bowlquet.) Yeah, it's new . . . it's from France. It's what they call a *sporting hybrid*. They're doing it all over Europe. All the rock stars and supermodels are doing it, too. You'll see it catching on here in, like, three months.

Here's how it works. You will design and install a miniature golf course with my super new hybrid Bowlquet game-making kit and—*this is the best part*—you get to create your own fun games and rules. Do you use a croquet set or a putter? Who cares? With my game-maker, you can use any ball and club combination! You may ask, "Hey, Eric, can we use a soccer ball and kick it through the course or some international lawn bowling technique?" Why sure you can—you're only limited by your imagination!

MATERIALS LIST

- 12 sheets of 16" x 12" x ⅛" thick foam in an array of colors (available at craft stores)
- A ton of imagination
- Indelible markers
- 50' chain-link fence to keep your entire town from trying to muscle in on your Bowlquet tournaments
- Twenty-four 3' redwood garden stakes

TOOLS

- Scissors
- Staple gun
- Hammer (to pound in stakes)
- Safety glasses

1. Take a deep breath . . . then exhale. Ready? Now, let the creativity flow from your being. The basic instructions for designing the Bowlquet game area are to first plot out a piece of unused lawn. Next you will create a series of 10 or 12 fun, yet challenging, obstacles for your players to enjoy.

Note: Depending on the area you have to work with, the actual number of obstacles can be adjusted up or down.

2. First, sit down with your kids, the foam sheets, scissors, and indelible markers. Draw, cut, shape, fringe, write words, design. Each sheet will be designed to represent one obstacle. Change the goals for each one . . . hit this, win another turn . . . this one, go back to start. Pick a theme: castle keep, soccer savvy, or land sharks. You can even make it educational in a sneaky way, by assigning each obstacle a number. Add the numbers together and the highest total score is the winner.

3. Once you have designed the foam sheets, attach the sheets to the garden stakes. Make sure you attach the foam sheet high enough on the stake to allow for the stake to be pounded into the ground and still have room for the size of balls you want to play with.

4. Install the stakes in the ground in a fun and (hopefully) silly formation and wait for the craziness to begin.

Stromer Slick Tip: To spread the fun around and allow for the greatest number of kids to play, you should consider handicapping the older and more adept children, by asking them to play with their nondominant hand, or play on their knees, or even play blindfolded, as long as they aren't in any danger of running into anything or each other.

Eric's Final Advice

LIFE HAS GOTTEN a lot faster since I was a kid. I bet you feel the same way.

Through the process of creating this book, I came to realize the importance of infusing some "low-tech" into my life. Now, don't get me wrong, I enjoy the latest technology more than most, but there is a simple beauty to working with your hands that a remote control can't seem to replicate.

I know of no computer game or TV show that can simulate the feeling of a power tool. And, by the same token, there is no substitute for family togetherness and the feeling of creating—not only the special moments, but the special *things* that bring you together as a family.

Take some time to experience each other by way of a family project. Instead of sitting around the TV or computer waiting for the handyman to show up in your lives . . . become the handyman, handywoman, or handykid that lives inside you. Be a Do-It-Yourself Family! Fix it together! Teach your children by doing and watch them become who they are. And if it all works out to be too good to be true . . . name the next one after me!

ABOUT THE AUTHOR

Eric Stromer, named one of *People* Magazine's "Sexiest Men Alive" and iparenting's "father of the month," created clean-up solutions for TLC's *Clean Sweep*—on which he has solved problems in over 250 rooms and remodeled nearly 50 homes! In fall 2005, Eric also starred in NBC's primetime show, *Three Wishes,* the much-heralded series designed to grant wishes and inspire hope to families and communities across America, co-hosted by Grammy-winner Amy Grant.

Eric studied theater at the University of Colorado, where he began work in construction to make ends meet. Upon graduation, Eric moved to Los Angeles, where he began remodeling houses. His eye for design and great craftsmanship captured the attention of celebrity clients like Mel Gibson, Elijah Wood, and Dylan McDermott, among others. Eventually, Eric landed a role in the soap opera *Santa Barbara,* and his new career in front of the camera was born.

Eric is the father of two boys and a husband to an accomplished and busy woman. Following his own dad's example, Eric brings his family closer together by engaging in building projects as a team.